THE LORD'S PRAYER
Through Primitive Eyes

THE LORD'S PRAYER

Through Primitive Eyes

A Stone Age People's Journey

GOTTFRIED OOSTERWAL

Pacific Press® Publishing Association
Nampa, Idaho
Oshawa, Ontario, Canada
www.pacificpress.com

Cover design by Gerald Lee Monks
Cover design resources from Dreamstime.com
Inside design by Aaron Troia

Additional copies of this book are available by calling toll-free 1-800-765-6955 or by visiting http://
www.adventistbookcenter.com.

Unless otherwise noted, Scripture quotations in this book are from the Revised Standard Version of the
Bible, copyright © 1946, 1952, 1971 by the Division of Christian Education of the National Council of the
Churches of Christ in the U.S.A. Used by permission.

Scriptures quoted from TEV are from the *Good News Bible*—Old Testament: Copyright © American
Bible Society 1976, 1992; New Testament: Copyright © American Bible Society 1966, 1971, 1976, 1992.

Scriptures quoted from NASB are from *The New American Standard Bible*®, Copyright © 1960, 1962,
1963, 1968, 1971, 1972, 1973, 1975, 1977, 1995 by The Lockman Foundation. Used by permission.

Library of Congress Cataloging-in-Publication Data

Oosterwal, Gottfried.
  The Lord's prayer through primitive eyes : a stone-age people's journey / Gottfried Oosterwal.
    p. cm.
  Includes bibliographical references and index.
  ISBN 13: 978-0-8163-2307-4 (pbk. : alk. paper)
  ISBN 10: 0-8163-2307-0
  1. Lord's prayer—Meditations. 2. Papua New Guinea—Religion. I. Title.
  BV230.O68 2009
  226.9'606—dc22

                                                                                        2008050726

09 10 11 12 13 • 5 4 3 2 1

DEDICATION

To the men, women, and children

Who pray and work with Christ

To make God known to all people,

Everywhere, as our true Father; and,

Who are crossing frontiers of

Culture, class, and community

To hasten the arrival of His kingdom.

A Word of Thanks

I wish to thank the people of the Tor, such as the Bora-Bora, the Waf, the Daranto, the Mander, and the Ittik for their hospitality while I lived and worked with them; for their patience with me, who at first seemed to them to know less than one of their children and who behaved accordingly; and for the many insights I gained from them while studying the Lord's Prayer with them. Among them were many pagan saints whose lives and insights have influenced me deeply, whose courage to be stands out as a model of living, and whose dedication to God and His mission has greatly inspired me. May the Lord continue to keep them and to bless them!

CONTENTS

The Lord's Prayer

Our Father which art in heaven,

Hallowed be thy name.

Thy kingdom come.

Thy will be done, in earth as it is in heaven.

Give us this day our daily bread.

And forgive us our debts,

     as we forgive our debtors.

And lead us not into temptation,

But deliver us from evil:

For thine is the kingdom, and the power,

     and the glory, for ever. Amen.

—Matthew 6:9–13, KJV

TO THE READER

I first learned to say the Lord's Prayer on my mother's knees in a language other than my own. In my youth I prayed it often, either in communion with others or as a personal prayer when no other words or thoughts came to mind. Then came the time of study at the university—theology and geology, anthropology and the history of religion, medical and health sciences. Long-held sacred traditions and teachings of the faith appeared less certain to me in light of my scientific studies. God appeared so much bigger, and my own inherited notions and beliefs so much narrower and smaller. I became aware of the frailties of human interpretations of Scripture—even those presented as "eternal truths."

In the midst of this struggle to keep the faith and grow in spirit and in truth, I received a beautiful card. On one side was that famous sketch *Praying Hands* by Albrecht Dürer, and on the other were the words of the Lord's Prayer. The card came as from nowhere. No address was given. No name of the sender. Just the words, "Don't forget this now." The experience has stayed with me to this very day.

As a result, I began a daily meditative study of the meaning of the Lord's Prayer, consulting the best literature on the topic at the time. These included Karl Barth's writings on prayer and the explanations given by the

Reformers, such as Martin Luther and John Calvin; the meditations by Dietrich Bonhoeffer while he languished in a Nazi prison; the sermons by Helmut Thielicke on "the Prayer that encompasses the whole world," delivered toward the end of the Second World War while bombs were raining down on his church; and the studies by Gerhard Ebeling, Joachim Jeremias, and Ernst Lohmeyer. Little did I know at the time how important these studies and the practice of reflectively praying the Lord's Prayer would become to my life and work. That began to become clear when, four years later, I found myself living and working among some seminomadic Stone Age people in the dense tropical forests of New Guinea, and they one day came and asked, "*Nana* [friend], teach us how to pray."

In order to be able to translate the Lord's Prayer into the native tongue of these people, I studied their language and culture and meditated daily with them on the meaning of this prayer. How does one explain the meaning of the kingdom of God to people who have no political power structures, who know of no institutionalized form of government, no rulers, no presidents? What is the meaning of "our daily bread" to people who know no bakery shops or grocery stores, restaurants or farmers' markets, department stores or factories—who every day go into the jungle to gather roots and grasses and hunt and fish in order to eke out a marginal existence (so marginal, in fact, that many of these tribes are constantly teetering on the brink of their existence, constantly in danger of losing their battle for survival)? What, really, is "temptation" to them, or the forgiveness of "debts," when they don't know of any monetary system? And what shall we say of "evil," when what they encounter every day is quite different from what we experience in our complex societies?

Every translation is an interpretation, so when new insights emerge, circumstances change, or people mature in their understanding, the translation needs adjustment or revision. But those people did learn how to pray personally and on the communal level. And their praying changed things. The following meditations show the nature of these changes and why they occurred, both in people as individuals and as communities. I am sharing them here both as a challenge and as an encouragement. The challenge is to deepen our understanding of the meaning of the Lord's Prayer, to reflect more consciously on what we are really praying for when we repeat the words Jesus Himself has given us, and to translate our reflections into action. For the Lord's Prayer is not only a summary of His whole gospel, it also is a call to action: a call to practice and to participate in what we are praying for—from the coming of God's kingdom to the forgiveness of our and other people's debts. This prayer offers us a road map for the mission in which every believer is called, enabled, and empowered to participate.

The encouragement stems from the fact that people's lives have changed visibly as a result of reflectively praying the Lord's Prayer. Fathers began to model their behavior after the Fatherhood of God. The will of God became the people's own will to follow, and God's forgiveness worked in them, moving them to forgive others. And what God brought about in the lives of these Stone Age people of New Guinea, He wants to accomplish in each of us.

What, then, is the message contained in these meditations on the Lord's Prayer? First of all, I hope the thoughts that follow convey the realization that prayer is a force to live by, to rely on—an empowering that enables us to live a fulfilled life, even when not every wish we have or dream we cherish is being fulfilled. It is important that we recognize our total dependence upon God, our heavenly Father, and make His will our own and that we do so constantly, without ceasing (1 Thessalonians 5:17).

Second, we need to understand that prayer must always lead to missionary action. That, in fact, is the very nature of the Lord's Prayer. The "hallowing" of His name, the coming of His kingdom, the fulfillment of His will that we are praying for demand that we ourselves are involved in these changes, that we participate in them. The gifts of God—and the revelation of His name, the coming of His kingdom, and the fulfillment of His will *are* God's gifts—these gifts always carry with them the intent that we share them with others. That applies to all His gifts, whether it's faith, bread, money, special talents or abilities, comfort, or love. We cannot truly pray the Lord's Prayer unless we share with others the message and the power that it contains. The very form of the address, " '*our* Father,' " indicates that the Fatherhood of God encompasses others as well as ourselves—those who do not yet know God as their Father and those who for a host of reasons no longer can believe or accept Him as Father. Nobody is excluded. That personal plural pronoun *our* also stands as a corrective to any form of racism or ageism, chauvinism or nationalism. The " 'our Father' " implies that we are all brothers and sisters, children of one and the same Father. And in a similar way, the term *our bread* indicates that while whatever God in His grace has given us is indeed personal, it does not belong to us alone; we must share it with others.

Third, besides an empowerment and a call to service, prayer represents the most intimate relationship between a person and God. In that intimate relationship, we stand naked before Him—the way we really are, without masks. No make-believe here. This helps us understand who and what we really are. It makes us aware of our weaknesses and needs but also of our values, dignity, and strengths. In Martin Luther's words, we recognize ourselves as both saints and sinners, weak and strong, without status and full of dignity at the same time.

I have presented portions of these meditations on the Lord's Prayer to Bible translators and seminary faculty in the Philippines, to missionary workers in many of the countries in Africa, Asia, and Central America, at retreats for ministers in North America, as well as in most countries of Europe, and more recently, also to groups of scientists and hospital workers. Long ago, an Australian friend and a German editor of a publishing company suggested at about the same time that I prepare these meditations for publication in book form. Twenty years later, after further study, prayer, and meditation, this suggestion is finally being realized.

May these studies help many to rediscover for themselves the meaning and significance of the message contained in this prayer that the Lord Himself has so graciously given us. May they reveal the power of that prayer and stimulate many to greater missionary service wherever God has placed them.

TEACH US HOW TO PRAY

It happened one day among the Bora-Bora, a seminomadic Stone Age tribe who roamed the dense tropical forests of the Upper Tor River Basin in West New Guinea. A group of tribesmen came and asked, "*Nana* [friend], teach us how to pray."

Their request moved me deeply and not only because of the obvious similarity between their request and that of Jesus' own disciples (Luke 11:1). The parallels went much deeper. The disciples of old already knew how to pray (see the next chapter, "How Then Shall We Pray?"), and so did these Bora-Bora tribesmen. In fact, their whole life was embedded in prayer. Before they went hunting, fishing, or gathering food of any kind, they would pray in their *kone*—a huge, conical structure located on the highest spot of their main village. The men would stand in lines opposite each other, often decked out in special costumes made of tall grass, leaves, and feathers; and they would pray by blowing their sacred flutes, dancing, shouting, and singing to the gods of the animals and plants and every other good thing. Every song and dance was a prayer.

When the men planned to go fishing or hunting, they would whisper a prayer for the fish to come up, or for the arrows to hit the wild boar at their *tempat mati*—a spot near the heart of the animal—or for finding little piglets that the women of the tribe could raise. It was hard to tell where hunting, fishing, and food gathering began and prayer ended. At times, they would ask their gods to forgive them for what they were about to do: kill animals for their bare existence. And they believed the lord of the animals—he whom they believed to have given them to the people—granted them that forgiveness.

When the women went out to beat the pulp of the sago palms and squeeze it in water to prepare it as their staple food, the men again were to be found in the *kone* asking the gods to guide the bats to plant more sago trees and that those trees would be filled with pulp. On special occasions, the men would pray for more children to be born, for floods and earthquakes to stop, for the sick to be healed, for protection from the powers of evil, and for the curse of death to be taken away. At times, they would also pray for the world to be restored to what it was before evil, sickness, and death entered it. Prayer encompassed everything these men did. Indeed, prayer was the very basis of these people's existence.

So these men did know how to pray. True, their prayers were more communal than personal, more corporate than individual, more formal and public than spontaneous and private. They were repetitious and often appeared to be rooted in the spirit of magic—the petitioners more intent on telling their gods what to do than on asking what their gods' wills were for them. Yet, their prayers did show genuine feelings of utter dependence and of gratitude—two of the hallmarks of genuine prayer. The men prayed from the heart honestly, with passion and holy conviction. And certainly the God of Abraham, Isaac, and Jacob, the Father of Jesus Christ, listened to them; Scripture tells us that " 'from the rising of the sun to its setting my name is great among the nations, and in every place incense is offered to my name, and a pure offering; for my name is great among the nations, says the LORD of hosts' " (Malachi 1:11).

These tribesmen knew of a Supreme Being greater, wiser, and more powerful than any other being, man or spirit—a Being who, unlike the other gods or spirits, was above all others and not limited to their tribe alone (Romans 1:19, 20; Hebrews 11:6). They had no other name for this Being than "Great Being" or "Great Being called upon."[1] But the apostle Paul's description of the people of Athens was true of them too: " 'I perceive that in every way you are very religious. . . . What therefore you worship as unknown, this I proclaim to you. . . . He [God] made from one every nation of men to live on all the face of the earth . . . that they should seek God, in the hope that they might feel after him and find him. Yet he is not far from each one of us' " (Acts 17:22–27). Prayer, indeed, lies at the heart of all religions, connecting people with God and with each other. People may be ignorant of God as our Creator and the Father of Jesus Christ, but God overlooks their ignorance and blesses them and cares for them (Acts 17:30).

First contacts

The Bora-Bora tribespeople asked me to teach them to pray just eighteen months after I first entered their tribal territory. I can't say that they were very happy to see me at first, to put it kindly. They were afraid, they later told me. Afraid of change, afraid of foreign influences, afraid of losing their culture and their religion, and thereby losing their identity and independence.

The first few days, they totally ignored me. They even forbade the children to come near me. I waited nearly two weeks in an isolated little hut outside the main village, praying that God would open a door. Things began to change suddenly and rather rapidly when Chief Oshemanya's only daughter by his third wife became very ill. She was suffering from a bad bout of malaria—the number one killer in these tribal areas. I cared for her, and God healed her. Other health care followed. Yaws—another common disease that manifests itself through large tropical sores—dried up in days after I injected people with penicillin. In their integrated way

---

1. *Owraitsja,* a word similar in meaning to the Germanic-Gothic term *Guth [Guþ],* from which our word *God* was derived.

of thinking, in which every part of culture is embedded in every other part, they promptly dubbed the hypodermic needle that I used the "Jesus needle."

Underneath one of the houses, which were built on stilts that raised them about a yard and a half above the ground, I discovered Nabak, a little boy who had been struck by blindness and paralysis. The villagers regarded this as the result of a curse from the god Nabarssof, who was greatly feared everywhere. The parents were supposed to abandon this child in the forest somewhere or offer him as a sacrifice to the evil god by throwing him into the fast-flowing Tor River. Instead, they had hidden him underneath their house, where they also kept their pigs. When they threw food to the pigs, bits of the food fell into the hands of this little boy, who thus had been able to survive. Nobody, not even the parents, was allowed to touch this stricken child, lest they also be "touched" by Nabarssof.

When I discovered the boy, I fed and cared for him—very much against the will of the people, who warned me that Nabarssof would strike me too. He did indeed, or so it seemed; for shortly after, I was struck by blindness and lost the ability to walk. This lasted for about a week. When I was restored to good health again, people began to ask questions about my God—who He is, what His name is, and what He does. They loved the Bible stories and parables because the villagers also communicated their truths through storytelling and parables, and because the physical conditions and life pictured in Jesus' stories in so many ways resembled their own.

Then one night, after a bountiful harvest of corn (*gandrum*) that I had introduced them to and taught them how to plant and care for, the men rushed into the *kone,* the sacred temple that had until then been the very center of their lives, and began to destroy the symbols and images of their gods. In a rage they shouted, "You have deceived us! You don't even exist." Then they set the *kone* on fire, turning that huge sacred temple to ashes, together with all the symbols, images, sacred flutes, and religious paraphernalia.

It was shortly after this power encounter that the men came and asked, "*Nana,* teach us how to pray." Their request was born out of the spiritual emptiness they felt after they destroyed their sacred house and got rid of the gods and sacred symbols that until then had been the core of their whole life—and not just their spiritual life. Their whole existence had been rooted in the beliefs associated with the *kone.* It had represented to them the universe, where they believed people were reborn again and again. Up till then, that place, that structure, had given their life meaning and power and hope.

Prayer changes things

Faced with this existential crisis, I decided to teach the Bora-Bora the Lord's Prayer. Together we began to meditate daily on the meaning of those powerful words that Jesus Himself gave us and that sustained Him in His own existential crises.

What a difference that prayer made! The Bora-Bora came to know God, our Supreme Being, as the Father of us all, who supplies us with our daily bread, who forgives us our sins and debts, and who is about to establish His reign of love over all peoples. As a result, they saw a whole new meaning to life and received new powers to live by and a new hope. A new vibrancy became the hallmark of this tribe. Formerly faced with extinction because of the utterly marginal condition of their natural environment, they began to grow in size and in numbers, in their economic endeavors, and in their social relationships.

Before, the tribe, like many others in the Upper Tor region, was characterized by a very low birthrate and a remarkable imbalance between the number of girls and boys born. In some areas, only one girl was born to every four or five, and in some cases, even ten, boys, leading to a terrible imbalance between the sexes that in turn led to strained social and marital relationships. Many a marginal tribe in the Upper Tor River area became totally extinct. Afterward, not only did the birthrate increase considerably, but the balance between the numbers of boys and girls born was also restored.

When the tribespeople were asked by researchers sent by the South Pacific Commission to what factors they attributed these changes, they answered, "Before, our life was empty and without meaning. Since we came to know Christ and we learned to pray to Him, life is full of meaning, bringing us happiness and fulfillment. That's why our women give birth again, and why again both boys and girls are born." Illiterate these people may be, without a written language, but still they are deep thinkers and philosophers. They understood the words of Jesus, " 'I am the way, and the truth, and the life,' " to mean not only spiritual life or life in the hereafter but physical life here and now as well (John 14:6). The apostle Paul has also reminded us that " ' "in Him we live and move and have our being" ' " (Acts 17:28). Christ, indeed, is the Author of life. He is our very life (John 1:4; Acts 3:15). Therefore, whoever has the Son has life indeed (1 John 5:12).

The Bora-Bora's economic conditions changed for the better too. Seminomadic food gatherers and hunters when I first entered their territory, they developed into a settled community—in fact, the largest in this part of New Guinea, with well over a thousand people in their main village, where before there were only one hundred and fifty.

In honor of the God they had found and to glorify His name, the tribe decided to build a new sacred house. They burned a portion of the rain forest to create "holy ground purified by fire," as they put it. Then they erected a huge building, tying the wooden pillars and beams together with rattan and rope from the jungle, as in the days of Solomon when the first temple was built and "neither hammer nor axe nor any tool of iron was heard" (1 Kings 6:7); and they roofed it with an overhanging thatch of long leaves folded together.

I asked them why they built such a huge church building when the whole tribe consisted of only some one hundred and fifty people. They answered spontaneously, "This house is not only for us. It will serve as a house of prayer for all tribes and peoples" (cf. Isaiah 56:7). And soon, it did indeed. Word of the changes in the life of the Bora-Bora tribe spread around the Upper Tor River territory like wildfire. Stories were told—often greatly embellished—about the good health of the people, the new size and power of the tribe, their crops, their changing birthrates, and their ability to get along with each other when before there were constant fights. Some people were so impressed with what they saw and experienced among the Bora-Bora that they decided to stay with them rather than return to their own tribes. And the Bora-Bora, once known for their fierce fighting abilities, became known as the peacemakers of the area, uniting tribes from two different cultures. When wars did break out—as they regularly did among these tribes—the peace negotiations that followed always took place on Bora-Bora territory, where people felt safe. Bora-Bora villages suddenly became villages of refuge.

Of course, not all fighting among the people stopped immediately. Some conflicts continued to burst out. They happened when Bostar's dog stole Dantar's fish; when Kaway beat up his wife, Beise, because she had let the fire go out; and when Ewan and a few friends introduced a new dance into the community. And a war between the Bora-Bora tribe and the Segar tribe threatened when Banneeh proved to be unable to give a sister or female cousin in exchange for his newly acquired wife as promised. But these conflicts differed from those of the life before in that the tribe didn't split, neither individuals nor families were beaten up or expelled from the community, and people learned to ask and to offer forgiveness.

The following chapters reflect the meditations on the Lord's Prayer that led to this New Guinea tribe's new life. It took me about three years to find a translation that was meaningful to them and to prepare the original meditations, and I made many a revision afterward. And still, each time I meditate upon the Lord's Prayer, new insights emerge, and I have new experiences with God, our heavenly Father. The condition for these blessings remains a person's willingness to be emptied of self and of old, long-cherished notions, practices, and beliefs, and a receptivity to being filled with God's power of grace through His Holy Spirit.

In meditating daily on the Lord's Prayer and translating it into the

Bora-Bora vernacular, I learned a great deal also from the people themselves about prayer. Born and brought up in the individual-oriented Western culture and trained in Western universities and theological seminaries, I was accustomed to seeing prayer as an individual activity, even in the midst of a community of believers. From the Bora-Bora, I learned the joy and power of communal prayer, as the Lord's Prayer really was intended to be. I also learned that praying is not limited to a special time or place, nor does it necessarily consist of words or songs. Its essence lies in a conscious and constant living in the presence of God wherever we are or whatever we do. Prayer is experiencing the reality of God every day and every moment—in times of our deepest need but also at the peaks of our joy and well-being; in times of decision making and when resting and relaxing. As the Bora-Bora told me when asked why they continue to pray so constantly, "Without prayer we feel lost, and our existence seems so meaningless, worthless, empty, and without hope."

Road map for mission

It is worth noting here that only two of the four Gospel writers recorded the Lord's Prayer—Matthew and Luke. A study of their versions of this prayer and of yet another slightly different form used in the early Christian community reveals that it not only was given as a summary of the gospel, not only as a means of personal comfort and empowerment, not just for communal solidarity, encouragement, and growth, but also as a model for all forms of prayer everywhere and for all time.

Matthew and Luke were intimately involved in mission. Matthew evangelized among his fellow Jews, while Luke worked among those of non-Jewish faiths, such as the Greeks. The differences between their audiences explain why these disciples gave us different versions of this prayer. In their endeavor to persuade people to accept the gospel, each of them, under the guidance of the Holy Spirit, adapted what they had received to the particular sociocultural and religious conditions under which they worked. The Lord's Prayer as we know it bears evidence to the fact that true mission strategy always implies adapting the message to the particular conditions of the people who are the recipients of that message. This strategy was also the hallmark of the apostle Paul's work. In both his writings and his preaching, he never grew tired of emphasizing that in sharing Christ's message with people of diverse cultures and religions, that message must always be shaped to the circumstances under which one labors.

A major theme of the reflections that follow is the powerful missionary character of the Lord's Prayer. At first sight, this focus may appear to be due to the missionary challenges that the prayer was applied to in the settings of these New Guinea tribes and to the missionary activities that the prayer inspired and empowered the Bora-Bora tribe to do. But upon closer look, it becomes clear that Jesus Himself gave this prayer to us as a missionary prayer, which clearly communicates His message, and ours, and points out the goal and means of accomplishing His mission. Scripture says the goal of all mission is to make God known to all creatures as our heavenly Father (John 14:6–11) and to bring about the kingdom of God in terms of its peace and justice, supreme love and happiness (*shalom;* salvation), and of its judgment of evil, temptation, and sin (Matthew 3:2; 6:33; 9:35; Luke 19:9, 10; Revelation 14:6–10).

Our understanding of the Lord's Prayer rests upon our understanding of Jesus' mission as a whole. We must understand and interpret this prayer in light of the entirety of His life and work, message and ministry. And in offering us an understanding of Jesus' mission, the Lord's Prayer also offers us a key to understanding our own. It opens our minds to the very essence of the gospel. While this prayer may be rooted in the Jewish beliefs and traditions of the time of Jesus' life on earth, it has also given us something totally new. That newness lies in His mission of glorifying God as our personal Father and in bringing about the arrival of His kingdom—that is, God's reign of love over the whole inhabited world.

No one can honestly pray the Lord's Prayer without getting involved in the mission of Jesus Christ, driven by the same love that also motivated

Him (2 Corinthians 5:14–21; 1 Peter 2:9–25). Praying this prayer consciously and with understanding becomes the antidote to both nominalism and ritualism, to vain and repetitive communal recitation without power, and to superficial forms of piety without involvement in Christ's mission. Praying it in the spirit and meaning in which it was given and in the mind of Christ (Philippians 2:1–5) will lead to a new vibrancy in believers and churches alike. It will bring new motivations and new actions towards church growth and the spread of the gospel to those who have not heard of it, have ignored it, or long forgotten it.

In the early church, all candidates for baptism received a copy of the Lord's Prayer, which, after their baptism, they recited as both their confession of faith and their commitment to share their faith with others. In the post-baptismal instruction that followed, the new converts were then given a fuller understanding of the words of this prayer and of its implications for their lives and their participation in Christ's mission (Matthew 28:19, 20). Nobody can consciously and with understanding pray this prayer without committing himself or herself to participate in word and deed in His mission of making God known to all human beings as the Father of all and of bringing about the kingdom of God in our lifetime.

Praying the Lord's Prayer, then, is in essence a declaration on the part of those who pray it that they identify with Christ's mission and pledge to participate in it with all their might, gifts, time, and talents. They thereby promise to the world that wherever they are, live, or work, in word and deed, by acts of grace and kindness, by calling for repentance and conversion, by promoting peace and justice, by caring in love for those in need, by working for a healthy environment, and by calling evil by its right name, they will make known the Fatherhood of God and the arrival of His kingdom.

The Lord's Prayer is first and foremost given to us as a prayer. And the deepest understanding of that prayer and its most powerful effects on our life and that of others come from truly making it our own and from practicing it "constantly," as Scripture tells us, "in season and out of season" (1 Thessalonians 5:17; 2 Timothy 4:2). As Augustine put it, "When we pray rightly and properly, we ask for nothing else than what is contained in the Lord's Prayer."

For Further Reflection

1. Prayer lies at the heart of all religions: Hinduism and Buddhism, Judaism and Islam, Christianity and primal religions. Does God hear the prayers of those who do not know Him as the Father of us all and who worship Him ignorantly? Explain.

2. What are the differences between praying from the heart and praying from the mind? Which of these two most characterizes your prayers?

3. Are your prayers characterized more by a speaking *to* God than a speaking *with* God—more by a monologue than a dialogue that emphasizes careful listening as well as speaking? What could you do to change that?

4. Prayer is God's gift to humanity, but like any of God's gifts, we must accept it, appropriate it for ourselves, and then share it with others. How does this apply to the gift of the Lord's Prayer?

5. We *are* the way we pray. How does the Lord's Prayer differ from all other known prayers of humanity? In what way can it serve as a model for all human prayers?

HOW THEN SHALL WE PRAY?

The apostle Paul told the believers in the ancient city of Rome that "we do not know how to pray as we ought" (Romans 8:26). But then he immediately assured them that we don't need to worry about exactly what we should say or how to formulate our thoughts and praises and confessions and petitions because "the Spirit himself intercedes for us with sighs too deep for words. And he who searches the hearts of men knows what is the mind of the Spirit, because the Spirit intercedes for the saints according to the will of God" (Romans 8:26, 27).

We hear something similar from Jesus Himself. When He walked the earth, it was customary for people to stand in public places at the three main hours of prayer and surrounded by many others, lift their arms into the air with the palms of their hands raised heavenward to show their piety and devotion. Onlookers may have been impressed by these people's spirituality, but Jesus branded it hypocrisy. It's not the words that count or the formulas or forms, but our attitude—our spirit and state of mind. " 'When you pray,' " He tells us, " 'you must not be like the hypocrites; for they love to stand and to pray in the synagogues and at the street corners, that they may be seen by men. Truly, I say to you, they have received their reward. But when you pray, go into your room and shut the door and pray to your Father who is in secret; and your Father who sees in secret will reward you' " (Matthew 6:5, 6).

Jesus also counsels us not to " 'heap up empty phrases' " or use a stream of words (verses 7, 8). In His prayer then, He's not intending to give us a formula or a standard prayer for every occasion nor a routine recitation of a holy text or a pious liturgy required for communal worship. He has designed His prayer as a model—given in outline form as the rabbis in His time all did—for every believer on how to enter into the presence of God as their Father in an attitude of trust and humble dependence upon Him. The Lord's Prayer is an invitation from God for us to participate in His rule and reign of love here and now, as well as in the world to come. It represents a continuous dialogue between God and His people—a celebration of our salvation and our relationship with Him as our Father.

This is not to say that right words and the form in which they are uttered are unimportant. Why else would Jesus have given us specific words and put those words in a specific form? Both are, like prayer itself, a gift from God, who has guarded this prayer till this day simply because He is anxious for us to be and remain part of His kingdom. He "desires all men to be saved and to come to the knowledge of the truth" (1 Timothy 2:4). The Lord's Prayer is like a protective shield around us, a lifeline, a tie that binds us to God. He has given it to us as a comforter and a source of strength. It is a refuge and a promise that—like all other gifts and calls from God—are irrevocable (Romans 11:29).

The disciples' request

Luke tells us in his Gospel that one day Jesus "was praying in a certain place, and when he ceased, one of his disciples said to him, 'Lord, teach us to pray, as John taught his disciples' " (Luke 11:1).

Why the request? These disciples were believers—followers of Christ. They knew how to pray. They were Jewish men who from childhood on had learned to pray three times each day: at 9:00 A.M., noon, and 3:00 P.M. They prayed from memory the *Shema,* in which believers pledged to give their love and wholehearted devotion to the one and only God and to meditate upon His law, and in which they rehearsed the blessings for obeying and the curses for disobeying God's commandments. They also prayed the *Shemoneh 'esreh,* the "eighteen"—a liturgical prayer that originally consisted of eighteen short prayers appealing to God for His mercy and favor. Many of them also knew the Psalms by heart and prayed them together with prayers of thanksgiving before meals and for special occasions.

They also prayed a host of ritual and communal prayers, one of the most important of which was the *Kaddish,* the proclamation of the sanctity of God. At the time of Jesus, this prayer was recited in response to the readings and explanation of a biblical text, the *Haggadah.* It started with the words: "Glorified and hallowed be His great name in the world which He created according to His will, and may His kingdom come in your lifetime and in your days . . . speedily and soon." This prayer—though spoken mostly at memorial services and in a much longer form—is still highly honored in Judaism and deeply anchored in Israel's soul.

Yes, the disciples knew how to pray, and they did pray. Why, then, did they say they wanted to learn how to pray?

We can deduce two main reasons for their request from the text itself. The first is the way Jesus Himself prayed. The text says that one day when Jesus was praying, one of His disciples requested, " 'Lord, teach us to pray' " (Luke 11:1). The disciples became aware of the enormous differences between their way of praying and the way Jesus prayed.

We know that Jesus often was alone when He prayed—away from people but also from the worldly noises that surround us everywhere. Away also from the sacred places of prayer and from the rituals associated with them. For Jesus, prayer was spontaneous, not tied to any time, place, or ritual order. It was always new and fresh, not bound by tradition.

Prayer was—and is—the most intimate way of relating to God. One stands before Him totally "naked" and alone. Jesus said that when we pray, we should go into our little "room" with the doors closed

(Matthew 6:6)—meaning that we should separate ourselves from the environment that normally stimulates and shapes our thoughts and activities. We should remove ourselves from our daily worries and obligations, interests and desires. This doesn't require a special place as much as it does a particular mind-set and attitude. For the disciples, as for many believers after them, praying was mostly routine, an honored duty, a ritual. It was mostly limited to certain times and places or special occasions. Their hearts and wills were not in it. After many years of repetitive practice, they hardly thought of what they were saying. Their prayers had become mere utterances of words, mechanical, something Jesus warned against in His sermon on the mount, in which He described it variously as "vain repetitions," " 'empty phrases,' " and " 'meaningless words' " (Matthew 6:7, 8, KJV, RSV, TEV).

Beyond routine praying

As all of us who have not given up praying altogether know, routine praying can easily deteriorate into a thoughtless, soulless, mechanical, and routine uttering of words. And then we are surprised when it remains so ineffective! That's what perhaps impressed the disciples the most in Jesus' praying—its effectiveness. He prayed, and He was able to multiply five loaves of bread and two fish into a meal that satisfied five thousand men, plus women and children. He prayed, and the sick were healed, the wind and the waves calmed down, and water changed into wine (Matthew 14; John 2). He prayed, and even the devil fled from Him (Matthew 4:1–11). He prayed, and He was enabled to accomplish God's will for all of us, so that the whole world might be saved and come to the knowledge of the truth (Matthew 26:36–46; 1 Timothy 2:4).

It is important to stress here that in all these events, Jesus acted as a human being, as one of us (Philippians 2:5–7). He had no powers that His followers may not also have through praying like He did! In teaching His disciples how to pray, Jesus offered them a way out of the often thoughtless, heartless, mechanical, and powerless forms of prayer. He offered them in thematic form a radically new approach that starts with God—*His* glory and *His* will—instead of being rooted in our needs and interests, thoughts and wishes. It's a form of praying that, with a feeling of utter dependence on God and a deep sense of humility, asks for His will to be accomplished. Such an approach centers more on listening than on speaking and is oriented more toward God's program and His intentions than toward ours. After all, our heavenly Father knows what we need before we ask Him (Matthew 6:8). Jesus Himself promises us that if we pray like this, He will grant us anything we pray for and empower us to do whatever He did on earth—and even greater things (John 14:12–14).

The second reason why the disciples requested Jesus to teach them how to pray, according to Luke, is expressed in the words in the same way " 'as John [the Baptist] taught his disciples' " (Luke 11:1). In the days of Jesus' ministry on earth, there were literally hundreds of teachers who, with their followers, wandered around the country proclaiming their particular message. Many of these teachers had a Messianic bent. Others were calling for a revival of the teachings of the prophets, while not a few were promoting movements of protest against the social conditions of the country or the occupation by the Romans. Jesus and John the Baptist were only two of them; other teachers represented the Essenes, the Pharisees, and the "Children of God." To make clear what their particular message and mission were and to distinguish their teachings from those of the others, each of these gurus had designed a special prayer that embodied their mission and summarized their particular message. That's why John the Baptist had prepared a special prayer for his disciples. Jesus' disciples wanted a prayer that would summarize their message and mission and distinguish them from all the other groups, sects, and cults.

And what a prayer they received! A summary of the gospel it is indeed. It also defines clearly Christ's mission and therefore ours. But it is so much more: it is a shield against the powers of evil surrounding us everywhere; a power to live by; an instrument of God's grace; and a source of happiness, peace, and righteousness. Martin Luther once described it as "an iron wall" that surrounds us everywhere and keeps us safe from the attacks of enemies and temptations—even doubt and unbelief. The Lord's Prayer tells us that we are what we pray. What a wonderful thought to live by! To all who pray this prayer with Christ, it gives their true identity: it tells the world who and what we really are as individual persons and as a community of faith.

One prayer—three versions

In the Bible, the Lord's Prayer comes to us in two versions: one is given by Luke (chapter 11:2–4), the other by Matthew (chapter 6:9–13). A third version developed later and has given the Lord's Prayer the form we are most familiar with, one that is prayed around the world among Christians of all persuasions in more than two thousand languages and dialects, including that of the Bora-Bora, Berrik, and Nadjabaidja in the isolated interior of West New Guinea.

Under the guidance of the Holy Spirit, Matthew placed the Lord's Prayer right in the middle of Jesus' sermon on the mount (Matthew 5–7). Literarily and symbolically, the Lord's Prayer constitutes the very heart and center of Jesus' inaugural address and therefore the very core of His message and mission. However, though the Lord's Prayer is prayed around the world and has been for some two thousand years now, few have recognized that it is the very center of a radically new ethic, a whole new social order, a new form of relationship between individuals and nations—indeed, a new world order. And those who have drawn this conclusion have commonly considered this call for a new order and ethic more as an ideal to hope for than a reality to be implemented.

However, from the beginning of His ministry, Jesus clearly announced that people who pray this prayer with Him should thereby also live up to the principles enunciated in His sermon on the mount: to be the salt of the earth and the light of the world; to act as peacemakers and champions for social justice; to love one's enemies; to show compassion to the poor and feed the hungry; to always speak the truth; to be faithful to one's marriage partner; and to refrain from judging anyone, which means that we should treat them the way we want them to treat us. There are no racists or sexists among those who pray the Lord's Prayer with Jesus in the meaning and spirit in which He taught it!

Many a government has forbidden believers to pray this prayer because of its revolutionary character and "subversive" nature, for this prayer does, indeed, have the power to change entire cultures and societies, and bring down governments and economic systems. And this prayer has inspired many a theologian to challenge traditional views of mission and notions of what it means to be the church in the world today.

Though the versions of the Lord's Prayer that Luke and Matthew gave have essentially the same structure and form, convey the same basic message, and share the same purpose and goal, the two do differ in a number of significant ways. These differences demand close study and attention because both these versions come to us as gifts from God Himself and because each of them emphasizes a particular message. Let's look at the texts side by side.

Matthew 6:9–13

"*Our* Father *who art in heaven,*
Hallowed be thy name.
Thy kingdom come,
Thy will be done,
On earth as it is in heaven.
Give us *this day* our daily bread;
And forgive us our *debts,*
As we also *have forgiven* our debtors;

And lead us not into temptation,
But deliver us from evil" (emphasis added).

Luke 11:2–4

"Father,
hallowed be thy name.
Thy kingdom come.

Give us *each day* our daily bread;
and forgive us our *sins,*
for we ourselves *forgive* every one who is indebted to us;
and lead us not into temptation" (emphasis added).

Obviously, Luke's version is shorter, as is the term of address he uses, "Father," while Matthew speaks of "our Father who art in heaven." Luke totally omits the petition, "Thy will be done / On earth as it is in heaven," as well as the petition, "but deliver us from evil." Where Matthew uses the words *this day,* Luke writes *each day,* and where Matthew uses the term *debts,* Luke uses the term *sins.* And finally, the version according to Matthew reads, *"As we also have forgiven* our debtors," while Luke has us pray, *"for we ourselves forgive* every one who is indebted to us." We will explore the meaning and messages of these differences later, in the different chapters dealing with these passages.

There is no question about the fact that it is Jesus Himself who has given us this prayer. Neither should we doubt the fact that Matthew and Luke were both inspired by the Holy Spirit to hand the Lord's Prayer down to us the way they have. The question then arises as to how these two versions developed in the context of the early church's mission and ministry.

Both versions developed in the decade of the eighties of the first century A.D., some fifty years after Christ was crucified, rose from the dead, and ascended into heaven. By that time, the message of the gospel had been spread all over the Mediterranean and had given rise to hundreds of house churches. Some of these developed among Jewish believers; others arose in the social, cultural, and religious context of the Greco-Roman world. As historical evidence shows, all of these newly developed churches attached immense value to the Lord's Prayer as a confessional statement of belief, a means of teaching the gospel and building the believers in the faith, and as a source of comfort and strength in the often hostile environment in which they existed. It was an essential part of the *Didache,* or "The Lord's Teaching Through the Twelve Apostles to the Nations"—the oldest Christian document other than the books of the New Testament, dating from the end of the first century A.D. In it, the believers are urged "after Jewish fashion" to pray the Lord's Prayer three times a day.

The third version

The version given in the *Didache* is basically that of Matthew, but it adds a doxology that reads, "For thine is the kingdom and the power and the glory for ever" (*Didache* 8:2). Our present version came about as a result of Martin Luther's Bible translation (1521–1522). Luther had found this doxology, which we all know now by heart, in a relatively late Greek manuscript of the Gospel of Matthew, and he considered it part of the original text. After his death, a number of Lutheran catechisms added these words to the Lord's Prayer based on the *Didache* but also because they were believed to be part of the original manuscript of the Gospel according to Matthew. Today, this doxology has become an essential part of the Lord's Prayer in all Christian churches, an ecumenical prayer of the truest kind.

Bible scholars believe that the two versions given in the New Testament developed side by side in the different contexts in which the churches found themselves: the one by Matthew connected with the Jewish-Christian communities in what is now the country of Syria, and the one given by Luke among the believers of Greek-Roman background. Some are of the opinion that both versions developed in their respective environments as part of these churches' worship, liturgy, and mission and that Matthew and Luke then wrote their respective versions as they learned it from the believers for whom they labored. Others, however—and they constitute the majority at the moment—believe that Matthew and Luke, as shepherds of their respective flocks and apostles of the gospel, adapted the Lord's Prayer to the particular religious and cultural circumstances under which they labored. Each version, then, is the result of a conscious and Spirit-guided attempt to relate the gospel to the needs and level of understanding of certain peoples in the context of their particular culture.

Matthew relates the gospel to people steeped in Jewish liturgies, beliefs, and traditions. His version of the Lord's Prayer shows remarkable similarities with the Kaddish—the announcements of the holiness of

God. Identifying the Holy God, who is so wholly other from us humans, with "Father," as Luke does, would be unthinkable and considered blasphemy of the worst kind. After all, the Bible tells us that for that very reason "the Jews sought all the more to kill him [Jesus], because he not only broke the sabbath but also called God his own Father, making himself equal with God" (John 5:18). Matthew, therefore, needed to add to "Father" the well-known Jewish notion of heaven, a status totally different from our human condition and existence. For those he sought to win, the closeness of God to humankind expressed in the term "Father" needed to be complemented by the proper distance implied in the term "who art in heaven."

In their own way, however, both Matthew's and Luke's versions teach us how we should relate to God and to each other. For if God is the Father of us all, and we pray to Him as *our* Father, that makes all of us brothers and sisters, members of one family under God. That applies in both Matthew and Luke to believers and also to those who do not know Christ. God is indeed the Father of all humans by creation and redemption. So, praying "*our* Father" affirms with the apostle Paul that " 'he made from one every nation [and race and people]' " (Acts 17:26). It also means that we thereby pledge to live up to God's ideal for His children, that we will consider people of all nations, races, religions, and cultures our brothers and sisters, that we will honor and respect them as such, and that we will share with them the wonderful message that God is our Father.

Similarly, we learn from both versions in different ways what it means to be forgiven and to forgive others. We learn to regard "debts" as "sins." We learn what it means to petition God for His will to be accomplished "on earth as it is in heaven" and to be "delivered from evil."

Matthew places the Lord's Prayer in the contexts of Jewish liturgy, worship, and sensibilities. Luke, on the other hand, starts from the perspective of the separation of us humans from God as a result of sin and of how God in His grace has bridged that gap. The challenge given by the differing perspectives of these two biblical books is obvious: for mission to be effective, we must continually shape the gospel to the needs, interests, and sensibilities of those to whom we wish to communicate it. The gospel as summarized in the Lord's Prayer must take on a totally different form when shared with Muslims than when shared with people of the Jewish faith or with those for whom prayer is meaningless or irrelevant.

For Further Reflection

1. How important are the forms and structures of our prayers compared to our attitudes and state of mind, our beliefs and relationships? How does the Bible describe those attitudes, beliefs, and relationships?

2. When Jesus prayed, things happened: the winds and the waves calmed down, water became wine, the paralyzed could walk, the deaf could hear, the mute could talk, and thousands of hungry people were fed. What would we have to learn from Jesus' prayer life to make our prayers this effective?

3. From the beginning of Christianity, the Lord's Prayer has played a prominent role in the church and in the lives of the believers—as a confession of faith and a statement of beliefs, a mandate and road map for mission, a mark of identity, a source of power, and as a unifying factor among the diverse groups of believers. What role, if any, has the Lord's Prayer played in your communion of faith (denomination or congregation)—its theology and teachings, mission and ministry, worship and walk of life? How has it affected your personal life and pilgrimage?

4. What is the meaning and significance of the fact that in the Gospel according to Matthew, the Lord's Prayer appears right in the middle of Jesus' sermon on the mount, that revolutionary inaugural address in which Jesus expounded His message and His mission?

5. What is the role of the Holy Spirit when we pray? (See Romans 8.)

Our Father Who Art in Heaven

Jesus begins His prayer with the words, " 'Our Father who art in heaven.' " Or, as Luke puts it, simply " 'Father.' " This term is not just a word, a label, or a form of address. It refers to a relationship, the very intimate relationship between a child and his or her parent. The God to whom we pray is not someone we don't know (Hebrews 11:6). We are surrounded by the evidence of His existence; we have seen His power, felt His grace, experienced His love. In fact, it is because of Him that we even are alive (Acts 17:28).

These words, "our Father," contain the whole message of the gospel. They give meaning to every other petition that follows. They are the key to our understanding of God's name, His kingdom, His will, His power, and His glory. They also form the basis of our own identity as children of God and constitute the very basis of all human dignity. This dignity is innate to all humans as creatures made by God and made in His image (Genesis 1:26–28), to those who do not or cannot believe, as well as to those who believe. In the words of the apostle Paul, "When the time had fully come, God sent forth his Son, born of woman, born under the law, . . . so that we might receive adoption as sons. And because you are sons, God has sent the Spirit of his Son into our hearts, crying, 'Abba! Father!' So through God you are no longer a slave but a son, and if a son then an heir" (Galatians 4:4–7). "You have received the spirit of sonship. When we cry, 'Abba! Father!' it is the Spirit himself bearing witness with our spirit that we are children of God, and if children, then heirs, heirs of God and fellow heirs with Christ" (Romans 8:15–17).

When Jesus taught us to pray " 'our Father,' " He thereby introduced something totally new—new to the people of His time, new also to us, and new to people of all religions and cultures everywhere. Something radically new with enormous consequences for our personal life, as well as for society at large.

The Lord's Prayer is indeed rooted in Old Testament tradition. There, God is also sometimes spoken of as a Father. Many other religions also recognize this characteristic of God—although with some critical differences. Even the tribes of the Upper Tor River Basin referred to the god Bonnanee as the Father of the tribe, the one who brought them their present culture and the things that make them happy. But there's a radical difference between the way Jewish and other religious traditions speak of God as their Father and the way Jesus taught us. In the Old Testament, the term *father* appears only fourteen times. In the four Gospels alone, Jesus Himself uses the term some 170 times.

But the real difference is not a matter of numbers. In the Old Testament, the term *father* is used symbolically and only in reference to God's relationship to Israel as a nation. For instance, Isaiah wrote, "Thou art our Father. . . . Thou, O Lord, art our Father, / our Redeemer from of old is thy name" (Isaiah 63:16). And Jeremiah pictured the Lord as saying, " 'I am a father to Israel, / and Ephraim is my first-born' " (Jeremiah 31:9). The entire Old Testament doesn't contain a single passage in which a believer directly addresses God as his or her personal Father. How different is the New Testament, where the word *father* refers to God 245 times! Jesus Himself sets the example, addressing God as " 'Abba, Father' " (Mark 14:36). In this testament, believers are also urged to address God directly as their "Abba, Father," and God is portrayed not merely as the Father of a nation or a group of people but also as our personal Father.

Moreover—and here's another huge difference between the Testaments—whereas, in the Old Testament, God is symbolically referred to as the Father of Israel, in the New Testament, God is spoken of as the Father of *all* nations, tribes, and people, individual and corporate alike! This was precisely the goal of Jesus' mission—to make known to all people that they have a personal Father in heaven and that they are His children (John 17:1–8). We are touching here the very core of all mission: to communicate by word and deed to people everywhere—people of all religions and cultures—that God is their personal Father and that He cares for them, loves them, and doesn't want any of them to be lost (1 Timothy 2:4); that He is a Father who is no longer an unknown quantity, a God far away, but He is One who has revealed Himself, is present in their lives, and is concerned about their daily affairs. He is a Father who suffers when we do, who heals us, supports us, and protects us. Anything else we do in mission is derived from these very words: "our Father."

A shocking term

If this idea of addressing God as a personal Father to us individually was shocking to Jesus' hearers, the word Jesus used to address His Father made it even more radical—even, in the minds of many, outright blasphemy. Jesus didn't use the Hebrew term *Abi,* which was commonly used in Jewish prayers and liturgy. He consciously chose the Aramaic word *Abba.* Unlike *Abi,* which bore a symbolic character and served as a metaphor, the term *Abba* was a common word used in everyday language that bore the feeling of the intimate relationship between a father and his beloved little child.

Actually, *Abba* is a diminutive term. To get the feel of this word, picture children who, upon seeing their father come home from work, run up to him shouting, "Daddy! Daddy! Daddy!" That is indeed the literal meaning of *Abba*—"Daddy," "dear Dad." Neither a metaphor nor a symbol, *Abba* carries the connotation of the trust and love children feel for their dad; the intimate form of a loving relationship.

The apostle Paul understood this clearly. He never substituted a Hebrew, Greek, or Latin word for *Abba* when he was speaking of God as our Father. Even when writing to the Romans and the Galatians, he always used this Aramaic term, for it contains the very essence of Jesus' teaching, the very core of His message and mission, the foundation of all Christian theology. (See, e.g., Romans 8:15; Galatians 4:6.)

There is still another essential meaning implied in the term *Abba*. It refers in particular to the feminine aspects of fatherhood, such as caring and nurturing; building relationships; showing compassion, tenderness, and concern; educating the children; and protecting them from harm and evil. This aspect of God was not totally unknown to the readers and hearers of the Old Testament. To the contrary, they were familiar with such thoughts as expressed in Deuteronomy 1:31, " ' "You have seen how the Lord your God bore you, as a man bears his son, in all the way that you went until you came to this place," ' " and Psalm 103:13, "As a father pities his children, / so the Lord pities those who fear him."

Yes, much of the Old Testament refers to God as being tender, caring, and compassionate—a loving Father who is concerned about His child Israel. Unfortunately, however, this notion of a loving and caring Father of the nation was lost during the years after the prophets spoke. The people's social and cultural notions of the role of a father as a patriarch and a rather superior, authoritarian being had clouded—even obscured—the more tender notions. Distance, obedience, and fear became substitutes for God's nearness, love, and tender, compassionate caring. Jesus saw it as His mission to restore in people's minds and experience the notion of God as our Daddy. No one in His day would have dared to address God that way. This was a new revelation!

But, honestly, are we ourselves not in a similar situation? Not long after Jesus gave us this new understanding about God, it again became clouded and even obscured. Over time, our own social and cultural views and experiences of fatherhood and masculinity have been projected onto the notions of God as our Father. The concept of God as a Daddy, a personal Father showing the feminine characteristics of being a loving, caring, and compassionate Parent, is as daring and revolutionary today as it was in Jesus' day. And so are concepts of His nearness and familiarity. Traditional cultural and social concepts have shaped many a Christian believer's notion of and experience with God. This has mostly happened very subtly and unconsciously, but it has happened—and to our detriment!

Learning to pray with Christ, "*Abba,* dear Daddy!" will bring about for many believers a revival of their faith and experience with God. Women need no longer feel excluded from the traditional masculine image and authoritarianism associated with God. They can find in the new revelation about God as our Daddy many characteristics associated with our Father that they can wholeheartedly identify with, aspects that they recognize in themselves, such as His caring and comforting, His love and compassion, His attitude of serving and being there for others—aspects that gave Christ His special authority!

The prophet Isaiah quotes God as saying, " 'As one whom his mother comforts, / so will I comfort you' " (Isaiah 66:13). Jesus was the express image of His Father (John 14:9; Colossians 1:15); and Scripture quotes Him as saying to Jerusalem, " 'How often would I have gathered your children together as a hen gathers her brood under her wings, and you would not!' " (Matthew 23:37; Luke 13:34). Praying with Christ the words "*Abba,* Daddy" will help bring about what Christ intended for His mission: the restoration of the kingdom of God in which there is "neither Jew nor Greek, there is neither slave nor free, there is neither male nor female; for you are all one in Christ Jesus" (Galatians 3:28).

" 'Who art in heaven' "

It seems evident for many reasons that in having us pray simply " 'Father,' " Luke has given us the original form of address. Matthew's form, then, " 'Our Father who art in heaven,' " is an adaptation of the message to the conditions and sensibilities of the Jewish believers with whom he lived and worked. There should be no doubt, however, that Matthew made this adaptation under inspiration of the Holy Spirit, and "all Scripture is inspired by God and profitable for teaching, for reproof, for correction, and for training in righteousness, that the man of God may be complete, equipped for every good work" (2 Timothy 3:16, 17). So, what is it that we may learn from Matthew's addition?

God is, indeed, our dear Dad. It is essential, however, to recognize that there are differences between an earthly father and God, even though Scripture, and even Jesus Himself, frequently makes the comparison (e.g., Luke 11:11, 12; 15:11–32). But the prophets also made it very clear that

"my [God's] thoughts are not your thoughts,
    neither are your ways my ways, says the LORD.
For as the heavens are higher than the earth,
    so are my ways higher than your ways" (Isaiah 55:8, 9; cf. Psalm
      103:11).

As the Hebrew people had done throughout the ages, Matthew associated the heavens with the place where God resides—where His temple and throne are. Mark and Luke, for instance, speak about the kingdom of God, which in the Gospel of Matthew is referred to as the kingdom of heaven. The Jews commonly identified heaven with the firmament, while using the plural form of the term, the *heavens,* to indicate a place above all earthly realities. That's where Matthew placed "Abba"—in the heavens. (The word is plural in the original Greek.) The message is clear: our Father is not tied to any physical place. He is above all things; He is everywhere. King David once asked, " 'Will God indeed dwell on the earth?' " (1 Kings 8:27). Of course not, he answered. Not even the highest heaven—that is, the firmament above all other firmaments; the sphere of the galaxies and beyond—can contain Him. That was also the opinion of King David's son and successor to the throne, King Solomon: " 'Will God dwell indeed with man on the earth? Behold, heaven and the highest heaven cannot contain thee' " (2 Chronicles 6:18; cf. 2:5).

Two things stand out in this Jewish concept of the heavens. First, God is everywhere. He is not tied to any physical reality; He is Spirit (cf. John 4:24). This concept emphasizes God's nearness, not God's distance, as many have thought. God is present everywhere: both beyond the galaxies and in a person's heart.

> Whither shall I go from thy Spirit?
>> Or whither shall I flee from thy presence?
> If I ascend to heaven, thou art there!
>> If I make my bed in Sheol, thou art there!
> If I take the wings of the morning
>> and dwell in the uttermost parts of the sea,
> even there thy hand shall lead me,
>> and thy right hand shall hold me (Psalm 139:7–10).

God is, indeed, present everywhere. And nothing, "neither death, nor life, nor angels, nor principalities, nor things present, nor things to come, nor powers, nor height, nor depth, nor anything else in all creation, will be able to separate us from the love of God in Christ Jesus our Lord" (Romans 8:38, 39). It is this nearness of God, our "Daddy," that is expressed in Matthew's term of address: "Our Father who art in the heavens." So, a missionary translation of Matthew's version for our time, shaped by the sciences of physics and astronomy, might well read, "Our Daddy, who is beyond all galaxies and universes, and who is near to us . . ."

The second aspect of Matthew's term of address is that God does indeed have a particular place in our universe somewhere beyond our firmament. Heaven is not some mushy, vague, elusive, and ephemeral pantheistic notion. It is indeed a place where God resides and where myriads and myriads of angels and thousands and thousands of other creatures serve Him (cf. Revelation 5:11). Jesus prayed to our Father at a definite location, where God's throne and His sanctuary are. Scripture says that when Jesus ascended into the heavens, He was seated at the right hand of God (Acts 2:33; Hebrews 8:1).

Chapters 8 and 9 of Hebrews further explain the meaning of this: Jesus entered a sanctuary in heaven not made with hands, where, as our High Priest, He is drawing people to God and saving them "to the uttermost" (Hebrews 7:25, KJV), working to establish His kingdom everywhere, ministering to keep people in the faith, forgiving our sins, showing mercy and sanctifying us, guiding His church in mission, supporting and encouraging us, fighting the powers of evil, mediating on our behalf, tenderly caring for all of us who have accepted Him as our Savior, readying the world for the day of judgment (Matthew 10:14, 15, 25; John 3:17–21), and preparing a place for all who believe in Him (John 14:1–3). That heavenly place is as real as Jesus is real—as the book of Revelation also assures us in so many places (e.g., 4:5; 8:3; 15:5).

What kind of a father?

The Bora-Bora tribe, like a few others in the Upper Tor River Basin, uses the word *ohwah* for "father." A few difficulties arose, however, regarding the use of this term to address God as our "Daddy." The questions arose because of how the people themselves experienced fatherhood. Would *ohwah* convey the right message? What image of God would this term project?

In our Western culture, the term *father* is a *descriptive* term: it denotes only one individual—namely the one person who is a biological father or who acts as a social father. We reserve it for one person only. Among the tribes of the Upper Tor territory, as in many other cultures around the world, the term *father* is a *classificatory* term. This means that this term is applied to a whole group of people. A person would address his biological father as *ohwah*. But he would also use that term for his father's brother, his father's sister's husband, and his mother's sister's husband—men who in our culture we would address or refer to as "uncle." Could such a classificatory term be used to convey the right message about God, who is One and Only, special and different from all other fathers?

This led to other questions: What did the people themselves see as the role and function of their *ohwah*? What was his attitude toward his biological children and the children of his brothers and sisters, who also are called his children? The questions arose because of the differing roles of the *ohwah* and of the *memmeh*—the term used to address or refer to a person's mother's brother. This latter person embodied the "feminine" side of fatherhood: a father's tenderness, and his caring attitude.

While a biological father was the authority figure in the family, the mother's brother would play with his sister's sons and daughters. The *ohwah* would teach his sons to become skilled in the use of bow and arrow and teach them to find their way through the dense tropical rain forests. *Memmeh,* on the other hand, would teach his sister's children the art of praying and would tell them the great stories of the tribe's past. The *memmeh* also would take care of the child when the child was sick or hurting, and he would receive the boys back into the tribe after their initiation, in which the *ohwah* played the role of teacher, life-giver, and judge. The *ohwah*'s relationship with his sons—his own and his brothers'—was rather authoritarian. He was the one who instructed them with regard to the technical and material aspects of life, whereas the *memmeh* taught them about spiritual things. It was the *memmeh*, not the *ohwah*, who joked and played with the children. A child would also inherit from his *memmeh*, not from his *ohwah*.

After I had been adopted into the tribe and had participated in some of their initiation ceremonies, the people asked me, "Shall we call you *ohwah* or *memmeh*?" That same question arose over the issue of how to address God, our "Daddy." He encompasses both sides of parenthood, the masculine and the feminine. He is, indeed, our

Ohwah—our Life-Giver, Teacher, Authority, and Judge. But He also has all the characteristics and attitudes and functions of our *Memmeh:* He's tender, caring, supporting, and forgiving. The Bora-Bora people really respected their *ohwah*s, but they loved their *memmeh*s. They tried to imitate them both.

In the discussions about God, some felt that we should address Him as *Memmeh*—that Father who loves us and cares for us, who forgives us and sustains us. Others, however, were of the opinion that God is more like our *Ohwah,* who created us and sustains us, who is our Life-Giver and corrects us—even punishes us when necessary—all for our own good. The discussions lasted, it seemed, forever. Then, after much prayer, a group of men came up with a suggestion. "Let's call our Daddy in heaven *Ohwah,*" they said. "But since He is also our *Memmeh,* why don't we change *our* attitudes and functions and adopt a notion of fatherhood more in accordance with that of our Daddy in heaven?"

Powerful!

And that's what happened. The Bora-Bora indeed now prayed, *"Amohwah"* ("Our Father"). At the same time, however, fathers became much more involved in the caring aspect of their roles as parents—more tender in their relationship with their children, more playful. I saw fathers who before wouldn't have thought of caring for their sick children tenderly watching over them. I noticed that fathers began to play gently with their own children, as much as they did before with their sister's children and to teach their children how to pray. The Lord's Prayer brought revolutionary changes in people's family lives and social organizations. No, it didn't happen all at once, and many a conflict broke out over the issue, creating tensions between husbands and wives and between members of the extended family. But after a while, life in the villages did change for the better—more in harmony with God's will for His children.

It is true that such changes were easier to accomplish and to observe in those small-scale and less sophisticated societies than in our modern and more complex ones. And those Papuan tribes who lived in precariously dangerous situations were known for their ability to adjust. "Improvisers of culture" they have rightly been labeled. Yet the challenge remains the same. We, too, have been captives of cultural ways that have shaped our notions and experiences of fatherhood.

I was fortunate to have had a father who cared for me, who played with me, and who taught me how to pray. Many of my contemporaries didn't have that privilege. They knew only a father who, in a drunken rage, beat up their mother, who was never present, or who was an authoritarian tyrant and male chauvinist. Yet with the new understanding of who and what God is—our "Daddy"—we, too, can change and adapt our notions and experiences of fatherhood to bring them more into harmony and conformity with the biblical concepts and experiences. All too long have we—believers in all churches—projected our own cultural and social notions, as well as personal experiences of fatherhood, onto our heavenly Father, thereby making Him after our image and likeness instead of the other way around.

Praying to God as our "dear Dad," who is both *Ohwah* and *Memmeh,* Father and Mother at once—instructing and caring for us, guiding and sustaining us, showing compassion and forgiving us, teaching and loving us—will bring about a revolutionary change in our lives and that of our communities. Christ Himself prayed, " 'Sanctify them in the truth; thy word is truth. . . . And for their sake I consecrate myself, that they also may be consecrated in truth' " (John 17:17–19).

For Further Reflection

1. Compare and contrast the concept of God as our Father in the sense of His being Creator of the human race and Founder of the religion to which we belong with the concept of His being our personal Father. How important is it that we come to think of Him as our personal Father?

2. To address God, the Almighty Creator of heaven and earth, all-knowing and ever-present, as "Daddy" or "dear Dad," presupposes a very intimate relationship. Jesus teaches us that as far as God is concerned, that relationship does indeed exist. What can we do to develop and sustain such a relationship? Would you feel comfortable in addressing God either privately or in public with the words "Daddy" or "dear Dad," as Jesus has taught us? If not, why not?

3. Why cannot racism, sexism, ageism, or tribalism exist among people who worship a God whom they mutually address as "*our Father*"?

4. What is meant by the phrase "who art in heaven"? Does it reflect distance and God's otherness, or rather, God's nearness and presence among us? In what ways?

5. Compare the nature of the Fatherhood of God as presented in the Gospels and in the Lord's Prayer to that shaped by our own culture and social conditioning. What are the differences? Would it be possible and desirable to adopt the notion of fatherhood as presented in Scripture into our own social and cultural fabric?

HALLOWED BE THY NAME

The biblical notion of names is complex and very rich. Names stand for personhood, character, identity, self, being, and personality, and for status, function, and authority. So, in Bible times, people paid close attention to the ceremonial rites associated with the naming of a child because they believed that a person's name communicated something of that person's nature, abilities, character, and even destiny. They considered the naming of a child to be an announcement of an entire life's program.

So it is with the name of God. His name stands for His personhood and character; His true self, identity, and being; and His attitudes and relationships. God's name stands for God Himself—the two are interchangeable. God *is* His name, and His name denotes His presence everywhere, in heaven and on earth. This explains the great reverence for the name of God that we find in both the Old and the New Testaments.

Two facts about God call for special attention here. The first is that God has revealed Himself. He has made His name known to us. He is no longer an "unknown God," or a God who is hidden. He has made it possible for us to know Him, to contact Him, to experience Him, and to tell others about Him. It was to this end that Jesus came into the world—to manifest the name of God (John 17:6). That mission continues, as Jesus tells us: " 'As thou didst send me into the world, so I have sent them into the world' " (verse 18).

The second fact is that by revealing His name to us, God took the risk of its being abused and misused, polluted and profaned. Therefore, God specifically tells us not to take His name "in vain," and He makes it clear to all people everywhere that He " 'will not hold him guiltless who takes his name in vain' " (Exodus 20:7).

It would take whole libraries to hold the stories of the various ways in which we humans have abused or misused God's name. And there is no end to it yet. In the name of God, wars have been fought and acts of terror have been committed. In the name of God, people have been enslaved and held in bondage, oppressed and robbed of their free will, rejected, condemned, and expelled from their communities. People have misused the name of God for personal profit and for gaining power and attention. That's why Jesus said, " 'Not every one who says to me, "Lord, Lord," shall enter the kingdom of heaven, but he who does the will of my Father who is in heaven. On that day, many will say to me, "Lord, Lord, did we not prophesy in your name, and cast out demons in your name, and do many mighty works in your name?" And then will I declare to them, "I never knew you; depart from me, you evildoers" ' " (Matthew 7:21–23).

Another risk that God took by revealing His name to us is that people would simply ignore it or neglect it. This attitude infects all of us—we neglect or ignore His name when we don't wholeheartedly devote our lives to Him; when we live our lives as if God doesn't exist; when we don't care about what matters most to Him in this world, such as taking care of the destitute, preserving His creation, working for social justice, and sharing His name with others.

In what we're considering here, we are touching the very core of what it means to be religious. The word *religion* stems from the Latin word *religere.* This word is the very opposite of the word *negligere,* from which the English word *neglect* is derived. In essence, religion means being totally concerned; it means devoting ourselves entirely to the name of God and what it stands for. This is the core meaning of hallowing or sanctifying the name of God. So, praying the Lord's Prayer as Jesus did is not so much petitioning God for something, such as bread, protection, or forgiveness. Rather, the person praying is expressing a wish, a desire, even a promise to be religious in the true sense of the word—to be totally and wholeheartedly devoted to God, our heavenly Father, to make Him and His work our ultimate concern, our reason to live.

" 'Glorify thy name' "

In part, hallowing or sanctifying the name of God means magnifying His name—giving Him honor and glory, worshiping Him. In the traditional Jewish prayers, which Jesus knew well, these two or three verbs are often used together and even as parallels. The earthly tabernacle was sanctified by God's glory (Exodus 29:43). In the Kaddish, people pray, "Glorified and sanctified be His great name in the world which He has created according to His will." In John 12:27, 28, Jesus, His soul very troubled, turns for strength to prayer and says, " 'Father, glorify thy name.' Then a voice came from heaven, 'I have glorified it, and I will glorify it again.' " Many have therefore seen in the prayer " 'hallowed be thy name' " a parallel to Jesus' prayer " 'glorify thy name.' " *Glorifying,* then, may mean completing the mission for which God sent His Son into the world (John 12:26; Revelation 14:6, 7). So the prayer " 'hallowed be thy name' " may then mean, "Father, establish Your kingdom now."

Two more points deserve our attention here. The first is that the hallowing of God's name is something done by God Himself, not by us humans! It is not we humans who in one way or another can add to the holiness of God, who is already holy (Isaiah 6:3; Revelation 4:8). Nor can we fulfill this prayer for God's name to be hallowed by urging His followers to live holier lives. The holiness of the church as a community of faith is not the result of human action but of the work of God

Himself. The apostle Paul tells us that Christ is at work in order that "he might present the church to himself in splendor, without spot or wrinkle or any such thing, that she might be holy and without blemish" (Ephesians 5:27).

The prophet Ezekiel also expresses this message. He says that we humans can contribute greatly to the desecration of the name of God—the whole process of secularization bears witness to that, both in and outside of the church. But the restoration of God's holy name is an act of God Himself. "Thus saith the Lord GOD; I do not this for your sakes, O house of Israel, but for mine holy name's sake, which ye have profaned among the heathen, whither ye went. And I will sanctify my great name, which was profaned among the heathen, which ye have profaned in the midst of them; and the heathen shall know that I am the LORD, saith the Lord GOD, when I shall be sanctified in you before their eyes" (Ezekiel 36:22, 23, KJV).

Our prayer requesting God to sanctify His name clearly expresses a desire on our part for God Himself to accomplish His mission of making His name known among the nations and of presenting to Himself a holy church (Ephesians 5:27). The church, when active in carrying out its mission—letting its light shine before people everywhere, making manifest in word and deed the goodness of the Lord—certainly does contribute to people's desire to glorify God. But it remains a work of God Himself. "God is at work in you, both to will and to work for his good pleasure" (Philippians 2:13).

Many interpreters of the Lord's Prayer have maintained that the name of God will be made holy by evangelizing the whole world so that all people will worship Him and magnify and glorify His name. These events, too, are certainly worth praying for. And to that very end God Himself has called into existence "a royal priesthood, a *holy nation,* God's own people, that you may declare the wonderful deeds of him who called you out of darkness into his marvelous light" (1 Peter 2:9; emphasis added). But Jesus specifically said, " 'Hallowed [sanctified] be thy name.' "

This calls our attention to the second point—namely, the true meaning of the word *hallowed* in light of Jesus' whole message and mission.

" 'Holy, holy, holy' "

Many have interpreted Jesus' prayer, " 'hallowed be thy name,' " as a prayer that wishes that God's name be praised, honored, glorified, feared, and worshiped. Why then did Jesus specifically use the term *hallowed*? His term may be used in conjunction with these other verbs and sometimes used as a parallel to them, but it remains a term with its own specific meaning, which differs from the meanings of all the others.

We see a glimpse of that otherness in Isaiah's powerful description of God "sitting upon a throne, high and lifted up; and his train filled the temple. Above him stood the seraphim; each had six wings: with two he covered his face, and with two he covered his feet, and with two he flew. And one called to another and said: 'Holy, holy, holy is the LORD of hosts; / the whole earth is full of his glory' " (Isaiah 6:1–3). As the story unfolds, it becomes clear that this Holy God wishes also that we humans share in His holiness so that the whole world may know God and fear and honor Him (Isaiah 6:4–11). God's call to holiness is at the same time a call to mission. That is true for Isaiah; actually, it rings through the whole Old Testament. The call to believers to " 'be holy, for I am holy' " has as its purpose that the believers make known to all people, tribes, and nations the name of God and what it stands for (Leviticus 11:44; 19:2; 20:26).

The same is true also for the New Testament. As the apostle Peter wrote, "As he who called you is holy, be holy yourselves in all your conduct" (1 Peter 1:15). Or, as Jesus Himself announced in His inaugural address, " 'You, therefore, must be perfect, as your heavenly Father is perfect' " (Matthew 5:48). So, the holiness of God and the holiness of His name are directly linked to the personal holiness of His people and to their involvement in God's mission in the world.

The Hebrew word translated "holy" is *qadosh,* a word that denotes something that is marked off, distinct, separated, set apart, withdrawn from ordinary use. This word also implies power, which can either destroy or bless. In the Old Testament, this word, with these meanings, was used with God, the Holy One of Israel. It emphasized His otherness as well as the purity of His nature, and His great power as well as His relationship with His people. Hosea conveys God's words: " 'I am God and not man, / the Holy One in your midst' " (Hosea 11:9). We feel God's power in every aspect of life. In fact, it is the basis of all of life, human and nonhuman alike. God's holiness is revealed in the energy of His will, which is righteous (Isaiah 5:16) and merciful.

The term *qadosh,* "holy," is not limited just to God. It can be applied to many things: objects and times, occasions and people, places and ideas, animals and plants, rituals and practices. One powerful example of that is the Sabbath. " 'Remember the sabbath day, to keep it holy,' " the fourth commandment says. " 'Six days you shall labor, and do all your work; but the seventh day is a sabbath to the LORD your God; in it you shall not do any work . . . ; for in six days the LORD made heaven and earth, the sea, and all that is in them, and rested the seventh day; therefore the LORD blessed the sabbath day and hallowed it' " (Exodus 20:8–11). Physically, that seventh day does not differ in any way from the other days of the week. But God hallowed it and declared it holy—separate, distinct, marked off, set apart, withdrawn from ordinary use. And He gave a whole set of rules and regulations to keep it that way.

Why was that day hallowed? Two reasons are given: First, as a memorial of Creation. God Himself rested on that day after He finished creating the world and everything in it, therefore He declared it holy. Second, it was a memorial of God's mighty act that freed the nation of Israel from their bondage as slaves in Egypt (Deuteronomy 5:12–15). God hallowed that seventh day of the week so that day could remind all people on earth of His power to create and liberate and so they could experience for themselves every week the blessings such a remembering brings. For no matter where we are or who we are, we all stand in need of God's repeated acts of liberation and of creating in us a clean heart and a new spirit (Psalm 51:10).

So, *qadosh,* holiness, doesn't exist by and for itself. Rather, it serves a particular purpose—namely, to offer people a blessing variously described as peace (*shalom*), righteousness, grace, health and healing, rest, joy, and salvation. The setting apart of certain times, spaces, or objects had but one objective: to help people in their need and bring them closer to God.

The slaves and servants of believers experienced freedom on that special day, the Sabbath, and so did their animals. Strangers ceased being strangers on that holy day. The holy rituals brought people a sense of rest and peace through forgiveness. The priests, set aside for special service, served as instruments of God's peace. " 'The sabbath was made for man,' " Jesus tells us (Mark 2:27). God set it apart and marked it off for the specific purpose of bringing a special blessing to all. And had we all kept that day holy, we would all have been far better off in health, strength, and in our relationships with God, with our families, and with all our fellow human beings. All of nature, too, would have been preserved better! God declared that day holy for our total well-being.

So, institutions are sanctified to bring those who participate in them a blessing. God hallowed His church for that very purpose—to be a blessing, in every sense of that word, to the world into which God sent it. The apostle Paul wrote of the "hallowing" of God's church (see Ephesians 5:25–27) for the sake of its being a blessing to the world. The church doesn't exist for itself. In the words of Emil Brunner, "The church exists by mission as fire exists by burning."

The hallowing of God's name has the same effect. We pray that God's name be hallowed so that all of us, believers and unbelievers alike, can receive a special blessing. The Bible doesn't leave us in the dark as to what kind of a blessing God has in store for us when we pray, "Hallowed be thy name." Exodus 3 says that God assigned Moses to tell His people that God had seen their afflictions and sufferings and that He would deliver them from their bondage and lead them to a land " ' " 'flowing with milk and honey' " ' " (verse 17). He told Moses to take that message to the Pharaoh of Egypt, who was keeping the Israelites in bondage. Moses complained, saying, " 'Who am I that I should go to Pharaoh, and bring the sons of Israel out of Egypt?' [God] said, 'But I will be with you' "—a promise that He gives to each of us who takes Him at His word (verses 11, 12). " 'Be strong and of good courage, do not fear or be in dread of them: for it is the LORD your God who goes with you; he will not fail you or forsake you' " (Deuteronomy 31:6; cf. Psalm 94:14; Hebrews 13:5).

But Moses wanted more. "What shall I tell them Your name is?" he said to God. God replied, " 'I AM WHO I AM,' " or "I shall be who I shall be" (see Exodus 3:13, 14). In other words, "You can count on Me. I will always be with you. I am always the same loving Father. No matter what is ailing you, no matter how oppressed you may feel, how destitute, marginalized, and poor, I will always be there for you."

A little later, as a sign of the veracity of that promise, God revealed to Moses—and through him to all of us—His true name. Exodus 34:5–7 tells us that God descended to stand beside Moses "and proclaimed the name of the LORD . . . . 'The LORD, the LORD, a God merciful and gracious, slow to anger, and abounding in steadfast love and faithfulness, keeping steadfast love for thousands, forgiving iniquity and transgression and sin.' "

Here is the very essence of God—the meaning of His name, the hallmark of His character, the very core of His being. God is love (1 John 4:8). That's His name. He is gracious, merciful, forgiving, compassionate, and caring. He is our Liberator, Savior, and Redeemer. Our Dad.

Returning once more to the meaning of the prayer " 'hallowed be thy name,' " we can say with confidence now that this means, "Our heavenly Father, dear Daddy, let Your love and compassion, grace and forgiveness be felt everywhere in the world—in our hearts as well as in the hearts of all Your other creatures. And we hereby promise You that we will share Your love with others wherever You place us in this world."

"Teaching them to observe all . . ."

In translating for the people of the Tor the desire of all of us human beings that is expressed in the prayer " 'hallowed be thy name,' " three issues stood out. The first is that in praying this, we are asking God Himself to hallow His name. After some explaining, those people understood this issue, and together we were able to express that concept in their vernacular.

The other two issues were their concept of names and their understanding of the notion of hallowing, of making holy. Their concept of the meaning of *names* was much closer to that of the ancient Hebrews than to ours. In their culture, a name stood for personhood and character, individual nature and achievement, stature and position in life, personality and being. So parents chose the names of their children very carefully. In fact, so intimately were people's names associated with their personhood that a newly born child wasn't considered a human being until it had received its name. People there would abandon infants born with certain physical deformities or born as twins, which was considered evidence of a curse. Sometimes, they even killed these infants themselves. When I protested and called such parents murderers, they said, "We aren't murderers. This isn't a human being; it hasn't received a name yet."

Commonly, parents chose a very important individual to put his or her name on the child in an elaborate ceremony. In their thinking, the name of an important person guarantees the newborn child a great future, with a high status in life. Often such name-givers were requested to accomplish a difficult task before they put their name on the newborn. For instance, among the tribes practicing cannibalism, a man might be asked to kill a person from another tribe and to catch that person's soul in the form of the last sound he or she uttered while dying. The name was thought to contain that person's life principle, his or her vital energy.

In Bora-Bora, people could also be given a new name later in life. For instance, one man received the name Buaya (Crocodile) because he single-handedly killed a twelve-foot-long crocodile. Another came to be known as Dantar (True Guide) because when his fellow tribesmen were surrounded by enemies intent on killing them, he guided them safely back to their own village. And still another became Oshemanya (Peacemaker) because he was able to persuade a group of enemy tribes to settle their disputes over land and women and to make peace. People's names, indeed, stood for their character and personhood, their personality and achievements.

Animals were given names too. When the little piglets caught in the jungle were given a name, they were thereby absorbed into the family circle. Women would suckle these little piglets at their own breasts, and their children would then call that pig "brother" or "sister." When I asked them if they would eat the pig when it matured, they very indignantly replied, "Have you ever heard of a man eating his own brother?" They drew their boundaries between animals and humans somewhat differently from the way we do in our culture!

Because the people of that culture accorded such importance to names, God's name was of great interest to them. As they learned of His many names—such as Love, Mercy, Grace, and Compassion—they understood their meaning so much better than we do in our Western culture.

Most of these people insisted that they receive a new name when they were baptized. They wanted to distinguish their new life in Christ from that of the past. They searched their Bibles or their memories for the most colorful and, to them, attractive biblical names, such as Methuselah and Abimelech. As they don't make a distinction between male and female names and often lack the knowledge of the historical contexts in which these biblical names occur, girls frequently were named Abraham, Samson, and Nebuchadnezzar. In the newly established churches among the tribes, one also often found a confusingly large number of people who chose the name Peter, both males and females. Their argument for choosing that name was, "I became a follower of Christ through my brother. But I also have often denied Him in my life. I am Peter." Name and personhood are inseparably intertwined and interchangeable.

When I began my mission among the Bora-Bora, certain tensions developed. Conversion always includes culture change, and while some members of the tribe wanted change, others did not. So I was considered a cause of division among them—one who threatened their power, unity, and honor, and their very existence as a tribe. At that point, through a special ceremony, a woman named Waronne adopted me as her son. Then I was a brother or an uncle to them all—someone whom they had to tolerate in their midst. One chooses one's friends, but one has to endure one's relatives! Fortunately, in only a little while, most all of them came to accept me.

Later, when my and my wife's first child was born, we named her Waronne after the woman who had adopted me. But when the people heard what I had named my daughter, they were puzzled. Instead of feeling elated and proud, they were astonished, depressed, and unhappy. That, in turn, puzzled me. When I queried them about it, they asked, "Why did you give your daughter a heathen name?" And then it dawned upon me. They regarded everything connected with a life before Christ in the darkest terms and that applied with great force to their names, which stood for their personality, character, identity, and even their future. So, they always called my daughter by her second name, Christine—"follower of Christ."

Holiness and *oorroorbessee*

All the tribes in the Upper Tor River Basin have a word that comes very close to the Semitic term *qadosh,* "holy." Among the Bora-Bora, this term was *oorroorbessee,* which literally means to mark off, to separate, to withdraw from daily use, to set apart. The notion expressed in it is related to the Polynesian concept of *tapu,* from which the English word *taboo* is derived. So, *oorroorbessee* seemed a fit translation for "hallowed." The people knew of holy places and holy objects, holy times and holy events, sacred buildings such as their *kone,* and sacred stories that could be told only at sacred times and in sacred places.

But as our conversations about the meaning of *oorroorbessee* progressed, the differences between this word and *hallowed* or *holy* in the biblical sense came clearly to the foreground. For instance, *oorroorbessee* often means "forbidden, dangerous, unclean, don't touch," and "don't trespass." It also frequently has the connotation of being forbidden for women and children, or for men only. What is missing altogether in the connotations of this term as compared to *hallowed* is the relationship to the divine, the strong moral implications, and in many instances, the connection with a blessing or something good for all.

In times of severe crises, such as earthquakes, floods, or catastrophic epidemics that caused the death of many people, some of the "holy" rituals performed in and around the *kone,* their sacred temple, consisted of acts of "sacral homosexuality" and abandonment of the marriage vows in "sacral promiscuity." *Oorroorbessee* didn't manifest itself in separation from evil or from something that was impure or morally wrong, but merely in a separation of special acts, occasions, places, or objects from the ordinary, the common, and the secular. It is true that many of the people didn't like these sacral acts. They preferred not to be involved in them. But they felt that they were necessary as a way of creating order out of chaos. They fought chaos with chaos so that a new order might emerge.

It was at this point that we found a breakthrough in the translation of the terms *holy* and *hallowed.* The people did know of—or rather felt—the difference between good and evil, right and wrong. And they were very open to the teaching of a connection between God our Father and the notion of holiness. In their own way, they also knew of certain blessings that would flow from respecting holiness—in particular the holiness of God and what He Himself had declared holy, such as keeping the Sabbath, abstaining from immorality, and following Christ in sharing His gospel in word and in deed. So, they continued to use their own word for *hallowed,* but they used it in the new meaning it has in the light of Jesus' whole life and teaching. *"Ambosseneh djemmesseh oorroorbessee,"* they prayed. ("Make known the holiness of Your name.") In fact, seldom have I experienced a deeper sense of true holiness than in these tribes after they had accepted Christ as their Savior and Lord and had committed themselves to share in His mission to pray for the outpouring and realization of God's love, mercy, righteousness, and justice among all nations, tribes, and people.

One striking event in the life of this tribe may bring further proof of this. They began to build—without nails and iron tools like axes and hammers—a huge church in the dark, isolated rain forest of the Upper Tor River Basin for the specific purpose of its becoming a house of prayer for all the tribes in the region. During its construction, Djeeree pointed out to me that one of the poles wasn't standing straight. It was crooked and leaning over. "Will God be angry with us?" he asked.

"Of course not," I assured him, remembering too well how they felt about their gods, who at times could become very angry and punish people.

Other men and women, all very much involved in building this house of God, joined in the conversation. "Let's try and pull it straight," someone said.

They tried very hard—to no avail. The horizontal beams resting on the pole were far too heavy and didn't allow the pole to move.

"When the roofing is finished," another said, "nobody will see it."

That seemed to settle it—but only for a while. When the building was almost finished, Djeeree came again, accompanied by a few others, and said, *"Nana,* we must pull down that whole building."

"Why, Djeeree?" I asked.

"Because that pole isn't standing straight. It's still leaning over."

"But is it less sturdy, less stable than the other poles?" I asked. "Could it cause any harm?"

"No," they all answered.

"And remember," I continued, "now the walls are finished and the roofing is in place, nobody can see that pole leaning over."

Djeeree and the others were quiet for a moment. Then Djeeree said, "But did you not tell us that God sees everything?"

Two days later, in the darkness of the night, when I was sound asleep, the men and women who for weeks on end had done nothing but work on the house of God—who hadn't gone out to gather food all that time and who were hungry as a result—pulled down the whole church. Not one beam remained upon another. By the time I woke up, they were already burning the walls and the roofing.

Tears welled up in my eyes. *What a disaster,* I thought. *Will they ever try to rebuild it?* I felt let down, forgotten by God and everyone else.

Then suddenly I felt the hand of Mooree on my shoulder. Mooree was a huge fellow, a rough-and-ready fighter who on many an occasion had led his tribe into war. "Don't be sad, *Nana,*" he said. "We ourselves are sad too. But you know, our heavenly Father is a holy God. He can live only in a perfect house."

I spent the rest of the day sitting on the bank of the mighty Tor River and meditating on the lesson these tribespeople had just taught me. We have Jesus' word for it that He and the Father love us and want to make Their home with us (John 14:23). And what do we do? We cover up, spin things around, wear a mask, deny, and play make-believe. These illiterate, Stone Age people showed me what it means to believe in a God who is holy and who urges us to be holy ourselves. "As he who called you is holy, be holy yourselves in all your conduct; since it is written, 'You shall be holy, for I am holy' " (1 Peter 1:15, 16).

The consequences

Everyone who consciously and with understanding prays, "Hallowed be thy name," becomes confronted with the reality of his or her own life in light of God's holiness. How do my own life, my way of thinking, and my actions appear before that holiness? Are they in harmony with Christ's prayer that God's love be made manifest to all people? We should become what we pray, showing to the world around us in word and in deed the reality of the Fatherhood of God, the Holy One whose name is Love, Grace, Mercy, Righteousness, and Justice. Does my life truly show the fear of God—in other words, the fruits of the Spirit by which God's name is honored, glorified, praised, and magnified? (Galatians 5:16–25; Revelation 14:6, 7). As the prophet Isaiah wrote, "They shall fear the name of the LORD from the west, / and his glory from the rising of the sun" (Isaiah 59:19).

It is important to emphasize here that in this prayer Jesus didn't have in mind primarily the realization of God's holiness at the end of time. We know that at the end of time the name of God will indeed be hallowed—shown in its full glory when at the name of Jesus, whose name is above every name, "every knee should bow, in heaven and on earth and under the earth, and every tongue confess that Jesus Christ is Lord, to the glory of God the Father" (Philippians 2:10, 11). No, Jesus was praying that this would happen here and now, in our time, in our situation, in our lives. " 'You are the salt of the earth,' " He tells us; " 'The light of the world.' " " 'But if salt has lost its taste, how shall its saltness be restored? . . . Let your light so shine before men, that they may see your good works and give glory to your Father who is in heaven' " (Matthew 5:13, 14, 16).

We often profane God's name by acts of carelessness, by pettiness, desire for power or money, pride of accomplishment, neglect of the hungry and the poor, and the failure to promote social justice. By participating in Jesus' prayer, " 'Hallowed be thy name,' " we commit ourselves to a new life of holiness, of bearing the fruits of the Spirit, and of making known to the whole world that God is love—He is gracious, caring, compassionate, and forgiving.

For Further Reflection

1. God's purpose in declaring anything sacred or hallowed—His name, the Sabbath, His people ("a holy nation"), or institutions or objects such as marriage and tithing—is for people to receive a blessing. What blessings are associated with hallowing God's name, keeping the Sabbath holy, being part of God's "holy nation," observing the sanctity of marriage, and setting aside 10 percent of one's income for the Lord?

2. How important is it for our prayers to begin with the wish or petition that God's name be praised, honored, glorified, and sanctified? What about that His name be made known, His mission be accomplished, and His kingdom be established both through prayer and through our actions?

3. In Scripture, the name of God indicates, among other things, God's presence among His people: liberating them and sustaining them, comforting them and forgiving them, challenging them and empowering them, creating in them a new heart and sanctifying them. Why, then, is the name of God so little known around the world? Why does He so often appear to be more absent than present, and more hidden than revealed?

4. Though God initiates and accomplishes the sanctifying of His name, in His mercy He has chosen ordinary people to participate in this task. Could not God have accomplished this better without us human beings? Please explain your response.

5. How can the petition for the hallowing of God's name best be realized in our world today?

THY KINGDOM COME

What did Jesus have in mind when He taught His disciples to pray for the coming of God's kingdom, and how did the disciples understand this petition? Though the disciples had been with Jesus for a long time, had heard Him teach, had seen His power, and had observed and even experienced His miracles, they didn't fully grasp what He meant by the prayer, " 'Thy kingdom come.' " Even after His crucifixion and resurrection, they still asked Him, " 'Lord, will you at this time restore the kingdom to Israel?' " (Acts 1:6).

Yet throughout Jesus' life on earth, the message of the kingdom of God and what that term meant had been the core of all His teachings (Matthew 4:23; 9:35; 24:14). Jesus explained it by His parables and demonstrated it by His acts of healing and a host of other miracles. " 'I must preach the good news of the kingdom of God . . . for I was sent for this purpose,' " Jesus said of Himself in Luke 4:43; and He sends us into the world for that same purpose (John 17:18; 20:21). This good news of the kingdom is mentioned more than a hundred times in the Gospels alone—ninety times from the lips of Jesus Himself. We still hear the urgency of this message ring through to us in the words Jesus spoke at the very beginning of His ministry: " 'Seek first his kingdom and his righteousness, and all these things [food, drink, and clothing] shall be yours as well' " (Matthew 6:33).

This message of the kingdom stands at both the beginning and the end of the Lord's Prayer. All the other petitions are enclosed by it, shaped by it, and find their meaning and fulfillment in it—from the petition for our daily bread to the petition for the forgiveness of our sins and debts and even to that for protection from evil! It is both the alpha and the omega of the gospel; it is the very foundation and goal of all mission. And it also stands as well at the beginning of all human history, determining its meaning and pointing to its goal and fulfillment at the end (Luke 1:33).

At the time of Christ, the Jews held a host of ideas about the kingdom of God. Some of these ideas had become obsessions and had given rise to a number of movements that attracted literally thousands of followers. Each of these movements tried in its own way to bring about the realization of its idea of the kingdom of God: some through political and even military force, others through rituals, prayers, and a return to the historic "faith of the fathers," or a strict keeping of the commandments. Some considered their Roman rulers to be the enemies of God who hindered the realization of His kingdom; others blamed their own Jewish leaders; while still others feared evil spirits, demonic "principalities and powers" not made of human flesh and blood (Colossians 2:15). What they all had in common was the notion that human action could establish the kingdom of God and that the time for it had come, as mentioned in the Kaddish: "May He establish his kingdom during your life and during your days, and during the life of all the house of Israel."

Central to the Jewish notion of the arrival of that kingdom in their lifetime was the long-cherished idea of the arising of a Messiah from the house of David. This Messiah, they believed, would establish a new kingdom by political and military force or by his spiritual powers. They looked for a kingdom in which evil had been destroyed, peace and prosperity prevailed, justice and righteousness reigned, and where God Himself was the only Ruler.

In the midst of these Messianic expectations, when the time had fully come (Galatians 4:4), Jesus arrived with His particular message of the kingdom—saying, " 'The time is fulfilled, and the kingdom of God is at hand; repent, and believe in the gospel' " (Mark 1:15). So, Jesus' message touched some sensitive chords. It sounded like the fulfillment of the Jews' long-held expectations and dreams, a realization of the promises God had made throughout the ages by His prophets, the beginning of the new age. Understandably, though tragic and regrettable, in many instances, the Jews heard that message through the filters of their notions.

Even Jesus' own disciples were the victims of this selective hearing. When He multiplied the five loaves and two fish to feed a crowd of five thousand men plus women and children as a sign of what His kingdom stood for—namely, God's concern for the poor, the marginalized, the sick, and the weak—the disciples didn't recognize it as such. They took the side of those who wanted to force Jesus to become King (Mark 6:15–32; John 6:1–15). They also sought for themselves the highest position in that kingdom (Mark 10:35–37; Matthew 20:20–22).

What happened in Jesus' time has repeated itself throughout the ages to our present day. Inevitably, our understanding of the kingdom of God has also been colored by the notions that have come to us through our social upbringing and religious heritage. So, praying with Jesus " 'thy kingdom come' " demands that we have a new experience of the Holy Spirit (2 Corinthians 1:22). Jesus said, " 'When the Spirit of truth comes, he will guide you into all the truth; for he will not speak on his own authority, but whatever he hears he will speak. . . . He will glorify me, for he will take what is mine and declare it to you' " (John 16:13, 14).

It was not until Jesus fulfilled His promise to pour out the Holy Spirit upon the disciples that they understood what He meant by His teaching and prayer regarding the kingdom of God and were prepared to share it with others (John 14:15–26; Acts 1:6–8). We have been given that same promise of the Holy Spirit (2 Corinthians 1:22; 5:5), and we need it as desperately as did the disciples of old. We need it so we can understand the good news of the kingdom and what it means when we pray for its arrival, and so we can fulfill our call to proclaim this gospel of the kingdom " 'throughout the whole world, as a testimony to all nations; and then the end will come' " (Matthew 24:14).

The gospel of the kingdom

In English, the phrase *kingdom of God,* or as Matthew called it out of reverence for the traditions and beliefs of the Jewish recipients of his message, the "kingdom of the heavens," is somewhat ambiguous. It suggests a territory or a nation or a political structure headed by a monarch, which is often associated with a rather autocratic form of government—undemocratic, without a constitution.

However, in the original languages—Hebrew, Aramaic, and Greek—the term refers to the act of governing, God's sovereignty, Heaven's reign. Jesus identified Himself with people's expectation at the time of a messianic King from the house of David who would reign in righteousness, but at the same time He declared that His kingdom is not of this world. In other words, His reign is totally different from that of any other ruler (John 18:36). His reign doesn't rest upon foundations of military might or economic resources, expansive territory or powerful political structures and institutions. The reign of God doesn't show itself in externals or material things. " 'The kingdom of God is not coming with signs to be observed; nor will they say, "Lo, here it is!" or "There!" ' " Jesus told the Pharisees (Luke 17:20). It arrives through what humans would identify as weaknesses.

Among those "weaknesses" are charity and compassion; an attitude of willingness to serve others; sacrifice and obedience; love of neighbors, friends, and family—and even love towards one's enemies; utter dependence upon God and a willingness to do His will; making God first in one's life; a commitment to justice; complete dedication to God; prayer;

a spirit of meekness, poverty, and peacemaking; honesty and humility; and a willingness to forgo revenge and to forgive (Matthew 5–7). The one who does all this and teaches this to others shall, in the words of Jesus, " 'be called great in the kingdom of heaven' " (Matthew 5:19). So, anyone who honestly prays for the coming of Christ's kingdom is thereby asking to receive all these attitudes and character traits.

The grammatical structure in which the petition originally was written (the aorist) calls for an imperative repetition: the kingdom *must* come again and again—it must come continually. Fortunately, God tells us, "I will continuously bless you and forgive you, heal you and redeem you, crown you with steadfast love and mercy, satisfy you with good as long as you shall live, and renew your youth like that of an eagle" (Psalm 103:3–5). What a relief is this promise that God will forgive us on a continuous basis! What peace and rest it affords by enabling us to live without feelings of guilt or shame and releasing us from captivity to our mistakes and shortcomings. What a joy to live by grace continually, as Jesus also invited us to do. " 'Come to me, all who labor and are heavy laden, and I will give you rest. Take my yoke upon you, and learn from me; for I am gentle and lowly in heart, and you will find rest for your souls. For my yoke is easy, and my burden is light' " (Matthew 11:28–30).

We receive the kingdom of God most easily when we become like little children (Matthew 18:1–5; Mark 10:15; Luke 18:17). Rich people and those of high status and position find it much more difficult; so do people whose lives are dominated by pride and pleasure, moneymaking and greed, or whose careers are built on evil principles and acts of injustice, or who outright reject Jesus as their Messiah and King (Matthew 19:24; 21:31, 43; Mark 10:23). And Jesus warns us, " 'No one who puts his hand to the plow and looks back is fit for the kingdom of God' " (Luke 9:62). To become part of that kingdom, we must repent and be converted, experience a change of attitude and a change of heart, followed by changes of those habits and practices that conflict with a life under God (Matthew 4:17; Mark 1:15). Some of those habits and practices, thoughts and ambitions may be morally neutral and legally acceptable, but when they hinder one from living a life devoted to God, they stand out as enemies of the kingdom. That, too, is what we are praying about when we pray, "Thy kingdom come."

The greatest enemy of the kingdom of God is the demonic forces who rule this world. So, their removal is a primary factor in the coming of the kingdom (Mark 3:22–27). This " 'prince of this world,' " this "god of this world [who] has blinded the minds of the unbelievers, to keep them from seeing the light of the gospel of the glory of Christ" needs to be dethroned from the power that he holds over people and nations alike (John 12:31, KJV; 2 Corinthians 4:4; cf. Luke 4:4–7; John 14:30; 16:11). Thank God, Jesus accomplished this when He came to this world and established His kingdom with power (Matthew 21:23, 27; 28:18). As the apostle John wrote, "The reason the Son of God appeared was to destroy the works of the devil" (1 John 3:8). Praise God, Jesus has extended His victory to His disciples as well (Luke 10:9, 17, 18)!

However, though Satan's power has been broken, we still need to pray continually that God will keep these powers of evil away from us. By Jesus' word and in His name we may say, " 'Begone, Satan! for it is written, "You shall worship the Lord your God / and him only shall you serve" ' " (Matthew 4:10). And as was the case with Jesus when He was severely tempted and "the devil left him," so the forces of evil will have no power over us (Matthew 4:1–11). This, too, will be our experience when we pray, "Thy kingdom come."

A process reaching its fulfillment

The kingdom of God, then, is a rather complex notion and experience. We hear that it has no external form, yet it comes with immense power. It is "within us," but it also operates in the world with glory and authority. We are told it has already come, yet it is still in the process of becoming and is therefore a reality of the future. It is embodied in the person of Jesus Christ, but it also exists as an entity of its own. It has dethroned the devil, yet he is still going around like a roaring lion trying to devour whomever he can and trying to blind people so they won't see and accept the gospel (2 Corinthians 4:4; 1 Peter 5:8).

A close study of the parables of Jesus—the vast majority of which are exposés of the meaning of the kingdom of God—confirms this complexity. The kingdom of God is a dynamic process—it starts like a little mustard seed and then grows into a full-blown tree (Matthew 13:31, 32). The kingdom of God is like seed sown without result unless it lands on fertile ground (Matthew 13:18–23). It is like seed sown without notice, which springs a surprise (Mark 4:26–29). It is like a field in which wheat is growing, but one that has weeds in it, too, which will be culled out only at harvesttime (Matthew 13:25–30). It is like a beautiful pearl to be purchased only after the buyer has raised the money for it (Matthew 13:45). It is like a wedding to which the father of the groom invites some people but then brings in others when those first invited don't come. And it is like a wedding for which some maidens prepare their lamps for delays while others don't prepare (Matthew 25:1–13). Often, the kingdom of God is present in small and even invisible features. But then it grows and matures and becomes a power to live by, a blessing for people, animals, and nature alike (Romans 8:18–25).

What stands out in all of Jesus' teachings about the kingdom of God is that when it begins, it is small and weak and not very noticeable. But then it grows into something huge and powerful, eventually encompassing the whole world and all who are on it. However, even while it is still small and seemingly isolated, it shapes the whole life of those who are affected by it, giving them peace, joy, a sense of meaning, and the certainty of salvation.

Perhaps a personal experience may clarify some of this complexity. I grew up in Holland—the kingdom of the Netherlands. The Nazis occupied that country during my teenage years, and they ruled it with an iron fist. Toward the end of the war, the Nazi occupation became very harsh. We lacked everything, and we suffered from humiliation, fear, and the loss of dignity and freedom. A blanket of depression covered us all; we were at a loss and without hope. Even our bicycles and radios had been confiscated.

Then, on June 6, 1944, while I was on my way to school, I saw a commotion near the church of the small town where I was staying. (So that I could escape the ongoing bombing of my hometown, I lived away from my parents and other family members.) In violation of the Nazis' rules, a crowd had gathered. They were hugging each other and shouting and crying. A man was raising an American flag on the steeple of a little church, and the people were saying, "The Americans are coming! The Americans are coming!" People were literally dancing in the streets at the news that the Americans had landed in Normandy—but only for a few happy minutes. Crack Nazi troopers immediately cordoned off the area and began to shoot—first the man who had been brave enough to raise the flag and soon randomly into the crowd. They loaded men caught in the melee onto big army trucks and took them away. Some never returned.

However, though we were sad and angry about the killings, we were filled with a whole new spirit. There was laughter again. Optimism took hold of us, and a new sense of dignity and hope. Though over time the famine became worse and the occupying forces' punitive measures became even more severe, the people were able to endure it. We knew that the Americans and their gallant allies had landed. D-day had come, and we knew that soon the war would be over and we would be free again. Gone was the depression that had burdened us all. We had regained our dignity, even though the realization of our freedom was still far off.

That's what the arrival of the kingdom of God has accomplished. Through Christ's life, death, and resurrection, we feel the power of the kingdom and experience the joy of redemption as individuals and as a community of faith. We may still be living under the harsh occupation of satanic forces, but their days are numbered. In Christ, we have become new creatures—children of God, citizens of His kingdom. We no longer live lives of depression, as if we were without God and hope (Ephesians

2:12). Our dignity has been restored, and we look forward with great anticipation and optimism to that day when Christ will return in great glory with myriads of angels—to that moment when God Himself " 'will wipe away every tear from their eyes, and death shall be no more, neither shall there be mourning nor crying nor pain' " (Revelation 21:4).

Christ and His kingdom have broken into this world. D-day has come for all of us; the decisive battle has been won. And though we still await that moment when Christ will appear on the clouds of heaven, we can live a life of freedom as citizens of His kingdom, and we can enjoy the power of His grace. This realization constrains us to continue to pray, "Thy kingdom come." In doing so, we're saying, "May this spirit of redemption, this experience of healing and peace, soon be fulfilled in its totality in the lives of all people, tribes, and nations."

Forever our Leader

To the tribes of the Upper Tor River territory, words like *king, kingdom, reign, rule, prince, governor, emperor,* and *president* had no meaning whatsoever. There were no rulers in those isolated, seminomadic societies. Those tribes had a very elaborate kinship system and social organization, but they had no political structures.

The tribespeople did live in continual fear of evil forces, and they experienced them daily. Their constant need for food and protection had created in them a feeling of dependency on a reality other than the physically perceptible one. They had an elaborate system of religious practices, rituals, and beliefs through which they sought food, health, and strength, the birth of more children, and control of the powers of evil in the form of spells and curses, sorcery, and magic powers. But they had no priests or shamans upon whom they could call to help them find release from their fears. They knew of no religious structure or organization either— no system that might be compared, even distantly, to a church organization. So, how could the gospel of the kingdom become meaningful to them—and a power to live by?

While these tribespeople knew little about human institutions, they were familiar with leaders. However, their leaders didn't acquire the position and then hold it ever after or pass it along to their heirs. In these tribes, all elevation to leadership was achieved on the individuals' own merits and skills. It, therefore, was also very temporary and limited to specific functions and tasks. When members of the tribe were going on a crocodile hunt, Buaya was their leader. He had proven himself able to kill crocodiles. When they were trekking through the dense tropical rain forest, Dantar was their leader. He knew every tree, recognized every sound, and was familiar with all the plants, knowing which ones were edible and which ones weren't. (And only a very few were!) On hunting expeditions, Bostar was the leader. He never returned home empty-handed. So, when I talked about Christ as our King and about His kingdom, I did so in terms of Him being our Leader. I talked about how He had achieved the position of leadership and what His leadership meant. That's how these tribes learned the meaning of the gospel of the kingdom.

The tribes of that region had a sacred story that they could tell only at sacred times and in sacred places. It was the story of a god who sacrificed himself by turning himself into an edible plant. When there was a severe famine—and that was almost a permanent condition among most of these tribes—this plant was the only food those people had. So their story was about a god who sacrificed himself so that people could live!

I used stories like this to make the tribespeople aware of the way Christ achieved His leadership—through the ultimate sacrifice on our behalf (Philippians 2:6–11). Though their stories didn't measure up to the story of the sacrifice Jesus made for us, I could use many of them as points of contact to prepare these people for the gospel of the kingdom.

I found another powerful means of acquainting people with the leadership Christ provides in recounting the parables of the kingdom. What eye-openers His parables were! These tribes communicate primarily through parables and stories. So to them, Jesus' parables were realities they experienced every day, not some story from another time or culture.

The parable they loved most was the one Jesus told in response to a remark a man made while seated at a dinner table: " 'Blessed is he who shall eat bread in the kingdom of God!' " Jesus responded to this remark with a parable:

> "A man once gave a great banquet, and invited many; and at the time for the banquet he sent his servant to say to those who had been invited, 'Come, for all is now ready.' But they all alike began to make excuses. The first said to him, 'I have bought a field, and I must go out and see it; I pray you, have me excused.' And another said, 'I have bought five yoke of oxen, and I go to examine them; I pray you, have me excused.' And another said, 'I have married a wife, and therefore I cannot come.' So the servant came and reported this to his master. Then the householder in anger said to his servant, 'Go out quickly to the streets and lanes of the city, and bring in the poor and maimed and blind and lame.' And the servant said, 'Sir, what you commanded has been done, and still there is room.' And the master said to the servant, 'Go out to the highways and hedges, and compel people to come in, that my house may be filled. For I tell you, none of those men who were invited shall taste my banquet' " (Luke 14:15–24).

The tribespeople wanted me to repeat this parable every day. They identified with it. "Are we all invited?" they wanted to know.

"Yes, of course."

"Is there really enough food for all of us?" they asked repeatedly. "Why did those people who were invited first not come? What excuses did they have?"

They couldn't identify with the excuses involving land ownership or earthly possessions. The tribal territory belonged to all equally; there were no individual landowners. Oxen and other domesticated animals didn't exist there. Plowing and planting was unknown among those hunters and gatherers. And they didn't have earthly possessions. They wore no clothes aside from a few tattoos and armbands and pieces of pounded tree bark. They had no permanent shelters. The one excuse in the parable they really could identify with was the one involving people's love life. But they could come up with plenty of other excuses as well, from envy and jealousies, hatred and anger, to stealing, lying, cheating, and adultery.

Eventually, they said, "We want your Book [the Bible] to be our Book. We want your people to be our people. We want Jesus to be our Leader forever—a Person who, 'though He was . . . God, . . . emptied Himself, taking the form of a servant, . . . [who] humbled Himself and became obedient unto death, even death on a cross' [see Philippians 2:5–11]. One who heals the sick, binds the forces of evil, protects us from harm, gives us food to eat, and gives us life here and now and will do so again after we have died. One who cares for us and forgives us. We trust Him. We depend on Him! Without Him, our life is without meaning and hope, empty and full of misery." So they prayed, *"Imkaradja banendees fortia. Amen."* ("May He forever remain our Leader. Amen.")

Yet another dimension

The kingdom of God, though present in us and around us and forever growing and progressing, is still a future reality. Therefore, we continue to pray that it may soon be realized. In many ways, however, that future realization is not merely an extension of what we are experiencing today. It is not only, in the words of the apostle Paul, "righteousness and peace and joy" (Romans 14:17). Not only divine blessings, pure and simple. Ultimately, the coming of the kingdom of God means the renewal of this world. The Bible speaks of a new heaven and a new earth, a new creation, new human beings, and a new covenant (Isaiah 11; 2 Corinthians 5:17; Ephesians 4:24; Hebrews 8; 2 Peter 3:13; Revelation 21:1).

The coming of this kingdom carries with it a negative, destructive element as well. To use the example of D-day again: the liberation of people from the yoke of the occupying forces meant the destruction of those who had been the oppressors and of those who had collaborated with the oppressors. The Bible speaks in this regard of a judgment. In Greek, the word used is *krisis,* which literally means "separation." At this judgment, those who have rejected Christ as their Leader, Messiah, and King, who have fought against Him, who have consciously substituted someone or something else for Him, or who have hindered others from truly believing in Him, are separated from the ones now fully liberated. As Matthew portrayed it, Christ our King, seated on His throne of glory and surrounded by myriads of angels, will separate people

"as a shepherd separates the sheep from the goats, and he will place the sheep at his right hand, but the goats at the left. Then the King will say to those at his right hand, 'Come, O blessed of my Father, inherit the kingdom prepared for you from the foundation of the world; for I was hungry and you gave me food, I was thirsty and you gave me drink, I was a stranger and you welcomed me, I was naked and you clothed me, I was sick and you visited me, I was in prison and you came to me.' . . . Then he will say to those at his left hand, 'Depart from me, you cursed, into the eternal fire prepared for the devil and his angels.' . . . And they will go away into eternal punishment, but the righteous into eternal life" (Matthew 25:32–46).

Other images—and we can speak about this unspeakable event only in images—compare the judgment with a separation of weeds from wheat (Matthew 13:24–30; 36–43), with the separation of the bad fish caught in a net from the good (Matthew 13:47–50), and with a court scene in which "books were opened" to separate the guilty from the innocent (Daniel 7:10; 2 Corinthians 5:10; Revelation 20:12). In every image given to us in Scripture, the separation of the good from the bad refers also to a punishment—a destruction of that which is evil. This applies to evil structures and organizations, as well as to "every authority and power" (1 Corinthians 15:24, 25), and to their human collaborators.

In the past, many churches and theologies postulated the existence of a hell (Hades)—a place of fire where all evildoers would be tormented throughout eternity. Today, we realize that the biblical image of hell is not of a place. Rather, hell means the total separation from God—from life, from this world—of all evil structures, evil forces, and evil beings, and then their annihilation by fire. Death is to be consumed forever too—and so is hell itself (Revelation 20:11–15)! How could we speak of a "new heaven and a new earth" if that renewed existence in "righteousness and holiness" would forever be soiled and spoiled, desecrated and demeaned by the presence of something that reminds us of evil and sin!

Isaiah portrays God as saying,

> "Behold, I create new heavens
> and a new earth;
> and the former things shall not be remembered
> or come into mind.
> But be glad and rejoice for ever
> in that which I create" (65:17, 18).

God's own righteousness and love, compassion and holiness, anger and forgiveness all point in that same direction. Even in His act of punishment, God shows mercy (Romans 11:32). "O the depth of the riches and wisdom and knowledge of God! How unsearchable are his judgments and how inscrutable his ways!" (Romans 11:33).

Through the judgment, our world—now distorted and deluded, deceived and dominated by "the prince of this age"—is made right again. All that is wrong and evil is done away with; chaos and corruption are replaced by a new creation in which God's love and righteousness, justice and holiness will penetrate not only all people but also every structure and institution.

> "He has scattered the proud . . . ,
> he has put down the mighty from their thrones,
> and exalted those of low degree;
> he has filled the hungry with good things,
> and the rich he has sent empty away" (Luke 1:51–53).

The theme of God's judgment has not yet found its rightful place in the discussions of the coming of God's kingdom. In the past, people have emphasized the warning aspect of this message: "Do this—or else!" Consciously or unconsciously, some people often used hell as a threat or as a way of controlling other people. In Scripture, however, the message of judgment is given as another invitation to accept the love of God in our hearts and to take our side with Christ.

When we pray, "Thy kingdom come," we're praying for the establishment of Christ's kingdom. Just what will happen then?

1. The coming of the kingdom starts with the return of Christ and the resurrection of the dead (John 5:25–29; Acts 24:14, 15; 1 Corinthians 15:12–58).
2. It spells an end to all injustice and evil, sin and revolt against God. Love will dominate our actions and thinking, our relationship with God and with each other (1 John 4:7–21).
3. Our relationship with God will be direct and without a veil between us. We shall see God face-to-face and live always in His presence (1 John 3:2; Revelation 22:4).
4. There will be no more sickness and suffering, no more pain or

anxiety, no more disappointments or despair (Revelation 7:17; 21:4).

5. Christ will be the center of this new universe with its new humanity. Our minds, nature, and characters will be like His; we will be restored to His image, reflecting Him in all we do and think. There'll be no racism there, ageism, or sexism (Romans 8:29; 1 Corinthians 15:49; 2 Corinthians 5:14–18; Galatians 3:26–29; Philippians 2:1–5; Colossians 3:10, 11).

6. This new world; this new life will last forever! God's kingdom is an everlasting kingdom. He will reign forever. All mortal beings and all things that are changeable here will have put on immortality and become unchangeable in the same way as God is immortal and unchangeable! (Psalm 145:13; Luke 1:33; 1 Corinthians 15:51–58; 1 Timothy 6:16; 2 Peter 1:11).

7. Not only will we humans share in these blessings that God has prepared for His children, but nature, too—the whole created universe—will be affected by it. For that reason, "The creation waits with eager longing for the revealing of the sons of God; for the creation was subjected to futility, . . . the creation itself will be set free from its bondage to decay and obtain the glorious liberty of the children of God" (Romans 8:19–22).

> The wolf shall dwell with the lamb,
> and the leopard shall lie down with the kid,
> and the calf and the lion and the fatling together,
> and a little child shall lead them. . . .
> The sucking child shall play over the hole of the asp,
> and the weaned child shall put his hand on the adder's den
> (Isaiah 11:6–8).

Preached in all the world

When Jesus came to this earth, He came to establish the kingdom of

God with the principles we've noted above. So, the kingdom we are praying for isn't a new reality. Nor is it a mere extension of what Christ has already established in us and about us. This kingdom of God had already been planned and established for all humanity from the beginning of His creation (Matthew 25:34; Ephesians 1:3–10). What we are experiencing now in the form of righteousness and peace, redemption and joy, are the firstfruits of this kingdom still to come—the signs of its reality. God invites us to live by these principles now—to find in them the peace made possible by the life and death of our Lord, to find in them meaning and certainty in life here and now, and the power to love even our enemies.

Jesus' message to us is the same as the one He gave to the disciples of John the Baptist when John was wondering if Jesus was the true Messiah or whether they should expect another. Jesus said, " 'Go and tell John what you have seen and heard: the blind receive their sight, the lame walk, lepers are cleansed, and the deaf hear, the dead are raised up, the poor have good news preached to them. And blessed is he who takes no offense at me' " (Luke 7:22, 23).

When Jesus sent His disciples to begin their work, this was their message and mission: " 'Heal the sick . . . and say to them, "The kingdom of God has come near to you." But whenever . . . they do not receive you, go into [the] streets and say, "Even the dust . . . that clings to our feet, we wipe off against you; nevertheless know this, that the kingdom of God has come near" ' " (Luke 10:9–11). Grace and judgment go hand in hand in our mission of proclaiming the kingdom and in our prayer for it to come (John 3:16–19).

We know we must pray for the coming of God's kingdom and pray for it continually. But is not its realization totally in the hands of God?

Yes, it is—yet the apostle Peter speaks of a "hastening" of the day of God that we can accomplish by living holy and godly lives (2 Peter 3:10–12). So do the other apostles. The apostle Paul emphasizes in particular our involvement in mission by proclamation, service, and building communities of faith (Romans 10:14–18). But, above all, we have Jesus' own word for it: as the Father has sent " 'me into the world, so have I sent them into the world' " (John 17:18; cf. 20:21). He sends His disciples to proclaim in word and deed the gospel of the kingdom as a testimony to all nations (Matthew 24:14; 28:18, 19).

Nobody really can honestly and with conviction pray with Christ, " 'Thy kingdom come,' " without actually wanting God to restore His kingdom now, in our lifetime. The people who pray this prayer are people for whom the kingdom is more important than anything else in life (Luke 12:22–31), who in their daily living show that they " 'fear God and give him glory' " (Revelation 14:7) through a life of holiness and godliness, and who are wholeheartedly involved in sharing the good news with those who have not heard it yet or who have heard it but haven't been able to accept it. In this sense, we are all called coworkers with Christ—people who, through the power of the Holy Spirit, join Him to hasten the coming of God's kingdom (2 Corinthians 6:1, 2).

For Further Reflection

1. The Lord's Prayer urges us to pray for and to participate in establishing the kingdom of God. That was also the very core of Jesus' message and mission. What then should be the first goal in our lives and the primary purpose of our mission? How can we best reach this goal and purpose?

2. What did Jesus mean when He said that the kingdom of God is "within" us? How can we experience the reality of God's kingdom in our lives, here and now? How does that experience relate to the coming of God's kingdom in all its glory?

3. What external and internal factors are hindering the arrival of God's kingdom in our time? How can we hasten the coming of God's kingdom? How certain are you that the kingdom of God will come—and come soon—in its full glory?

4. How is the line in the Lord's Prayer that expresses our desire for the coming of God's kingdom related to the previous line, " 'hallowed be thy name,' " and to the form of address "Abba," "dear Dad"? This prayer tells us that the kingdom of God is in fact our "dear Dad's" kingdom. What does this mean—what are the implications?

5. Are there any preconditions that we must meet to be prepared for the arrival of God's kingdom in full glory? What do these preconditions say about the kind of people we ought to be?

THY WILL BE DONE . . .

The third petition in the Lord's Prayer, " 'thy will be done,' " like the first two, " 'hallowed be thy name' " and " 'thy kingdom come,' " is God-centered. That's in contrast to the petitions that follow, which concern *our* needs: *our* bread, *our* debts, and *our* struggles with temptation. This third petition occurs only in the version of the prayer Matthew has recorded for us. Luke gives us only two "Thy" petitions: " 'hallowed be thy name' " and " 'thy kingdom come.' " Did Luke perhaps drop one of these petitions? Or did Matthew add one to the original? Or is there a third possibility still?

It isn't very likely that Luke could simply have dropped a petition that plays such a central role in Jesus' life and work. Jesus lived this petition! He embodied it. From childhood on, His whole life centered on doing the will of His heavenly Father. As a twelve-year-old child, He responded to the anxiety His mother expressed when she and Joseph had lost Him in the crowd with the words: " 'Did you not know that I must be in my Father's house?' " (Luke 2:49). And to His disciples when they expressed concern because He had not eaten in a while, He said, " 'My food is to do the will of him who sent me, and to accomplish his work' " (John 4:34; cf. John 6:38). Jesus' life and work—His whole existence—centered on doing the will of God.

Luke himself also tells us that he had in every detail closely and carefully researched what eyewitnesses and ministers of the Word had reported about the life and work of Jesus, so he could write "an orderly account" (Luke 1:3). It is unthinkable that a man like Luke would have dared to leave out such an important part of the Lord's Prayer—a sacred text that characterized Jesus' whole life and work. We may assume, therefore, that Luke, under the guidance of the Holy Spirit, has delivered to us the form of the Lord's Prayer that he himself received from "those who from the beginning were eyewitnesses and ministers of the word" (Luke 1:2).

Could it be, then, that Matthew may have added this petition to the original text delivered by the saints? That is not very likely either. We know that Matthew did shape his message to the cultural and religious sensitivities of his Jewish hearers. And doing God's will belonged to the highest and best in the Jewish religion; they did God's will not as a burden or a duty but willingly and happily. Psalms is full of such assertions: " 'I delight to do thy will, O my God; / thy law is within my heart' " (Psalm 40:8; see also Psalms 1; 119, among others). But missionary adaptations of the message go only so far. They are bound by the meaning of the text and its contexts. Matthew himself had heard Jesus say by way of introduction to the Lord's Prayer that it is not one's use of many words that catches God's attention. After all, He knows what we need before we ask Him (Matthew 6:7, 8). Moreover, Matthew was well aware of the divine warning against adding anything to the words spoken by Christ or the prophets or the apostles (Revelation 22:18).

We know also that both Matthew and Luke were engaged in pastoral missionary work: Matthew among the Jewish communities in what is now known as Syria, and Luke among those of a Gentile background. So, the message they proclaimed had to be shaped to the cultural and religious conditions prevalent in each community. Attention to the contexts, in which each of these pastor-evangelists has given us the Lord's Prayer, is revealing. It suggests that Matthew emphasized in particular what Jesus told the crowds, who had come to hear Him, about one's attitude when praying and the basic content of one's prayer. Luke, on the other hand, tells us that Jesus gave His prayer in particular to the twelve disciples, that He emphasized *how* they should pray, and that He did so in response to the disciples' request, " 'Lord, teach us [how] to pray' " (Luke 11:1).

Matthew, whose concern was for the Jewish believers in Christ, used a much-loved, ancient Hebrew form of poetry known as "parallelism." In this form of writing, the author repeats a statement in two or three different forms, each of which emphasizes a particular aspect of the concept or truth. So "Thy will be done" is actually a parallel statement to "Thy kingdom come" and even to "hallowed be Thy name." All three plead for the same thing—the fulfillment of God's plan for this world through the restoration of His reign.

It is very likely, therefore, that the Lord's Prayer has come to us in these two versions, with some specific missionary adaptations. Both versions seem authentic; they seem to have originated with Jesus Himself. Each of the versions, which Jesus gave on different occasions and in different contexts, was preserved in different communities of faith and later passed on to us in written form.

Knowing the will of God

In the original languages in which the Bible has come to us, the term *will* has a much wider and a more complex meaning than it does in our Western languages and cultures. This difference in meaning has led to a number of misunderstandings and misinterpretations of this petition, often with serious consequences for people's faith. For instance, throughout the Old Testament, words such as *counsel, goodwill, favor, deliberate plan, wish, desire, purpose, guidance,* and *good pleasure* are used where we use the term *will.* In the New Testament, the three Greek words often translated as "will" have the following meanings: God's eternal plan and purpose based on His counsel and deliberations, His inclination, and

His good pleasure or delight (Luke 7:30; Acts 2:23; 4:28; Romans 12:2; Ephesians 1:5, 9, 11; Philippians 2:13). Which of these meanings or what combination of these meanings did Jesus have in mind when He taught us to pray, " 'Thy will be done' "?

Before we look at this critical question, let me emphasize again that, as in the previous two petitions, Jesus—and we with Him and through Him—is petitioning His Father to implement what He is praying for. Jesus is requesting God to fulfill His will, just as He requested Him to hallow His name and to restore His kingdom. The petition expressed here finds its center in God, in His plan, in His "good pleasure," not in our needs or wishes. A good missionary translation of this petition for today would read: "Heavenly Father, please implement Your agenda."

This point doesn't mean our needs are excluded from the Lord's Prayer. Jesus has our needs in mind when He tells us to ask for our daily bread, the forgiveness of our sins, and protection from temptation. But all of these human-centered petitions are closely tied to and dependent on this particular petition, in which we ask God, our Father, to implement His agenda, to follow His plan for His "good pleasure."

And there is no confusion whatsoever as to what this plan, this divine agenda, really stands for—the salvation of us all. God "desires all men to be saved and to come to the knowledge of the truth" (1 Timothy 2:4). The reason Jesus came into this world was to execute this divine plan " 'to seek and to save the lost' " (Luke 19:10; see also John 3:16, 17). "In him we have redemption through his blood, the forgiveness of our trespasses, according to the riches of his grace which he lavished upon us. For he has made known to us in all wisdom and insight the mystery of his will, according to his purpose which he set forth in Christ as a plan for the fulness of time, to unite all things in him, things in heaven and things on earth" (Ephesians 1:7–10).

The mystery of God's will was hidden for ages (Ephesians 3:9). It wasn't new; it has existed from the very beginning of time (Matthew 13:35; 25:34). Many prophets and righteous men longed to see, hear, and understand it. God has revealed it to us in Christ (Matthew 11:25; 13:17; Ephesians 3:10–21), who worked "according to the counsel of [God's] will" (Ephesians 1:11). God revealed and accomplished His "eternal purpose" in Jesus' life and death (Ephesians 3:11).

The meaning of this petition stands out most clearly and most powerfully when we see Jesus, in agony and sweating drops of blood, crying out to God the very prayer He taught us: " 'Thy will be done' " (Matthew 26:42). At stake here was God's whole plan of salvation—our personal redemption and that of the whole world; the restoration of God's reign based on love and righteousness rather than on coercion. Satan and his followers have always maintained that a kingdom based on love voluntarily given and received in freedom isn't viable. God's agenda is to prove that it is viable, and in Christ, He did—but at what a price: the suffering and death of His own Son!

So, praying "Thy will be done" means first and foremost asking God to implement His plan of salvation in us and in all people for whom Christ has died. This is a missionary prayer if there ever was one! It also means that the ones who pray this petition with Christ and in His name "might live no longer for themselves but for him who for their sake died and was raised" (2 Corinthians 5:15)—and this in a double sense: in a new holiness of life, as one who is in Christ "is a new creation" (verse 17), and second, as one who has been given "the ministry of reconciliation" (verse 18). Praying this petition with Christ makes us all ministers of the gospel of reconciliation in the places and situations where God has put us, identifying us with the agenda and plan God has for this world.

What hinders God's will?

While God's will is already perfectly implemented in heaven, it isn't yet on earth—hence the prayer " 'on earth as it is in heaven.' " What is it that has prevented God's agenda, His plan and purpose from being implemented?

According to Scripture, two main factors are at work: a satanic one and a human one. First, the satanic factor. Tradition has it that when God decided to create us in His own image and likeness, the archangel Lucifer, a creature depicted in Scripture as

"the signet of perfection,
   full of wisdom
   and perfect in beauty" (Ezekiel 28:12),

protested out of fear that his position was being threatened by the new creature. Using the king of Babylon as a symbol, the prophet Isaiah described what happened:

"You said in your heart,
   'I will ascend to heaven;
above the stars of God
   I will set my throne on high; . . .
   I will make myself like the Most High' " (Isaiah 14:13, 14).

Apparently, a battle followed between the angels of God and those of Satan, and the former archangel and his forces were defeated. Revelation describes it as follows:

Now war arose in heaven, Michael and his angels fighting against the dragon; and the dragon and his angels fought, but they were defeated and there was no longer any place for them in heaven. And the great dragon was thrown down, that ancient serpent, who is called the Devil and Satan, the deceiver of the whole world—he was thrown down to the earth, and his angels were thrown down with him. And I heard a loud voice in heaven, saying, "Now the salvation and the power and the kingdom of our God and the authority of his Christ have come, for the accuser of our brethren has been thrown down, who accuses them day and night before our God. . . . Rejoice then, O heaven and you that dwell therein! But woe to you, O earth and sea, for the devil has come down to you in great wrath, because he knows that his time is short!" (Revelation 12:7–12; see also Ezekiel 28:12–19).

In our daily life under God and in our ministries of reconciliation, we are constantly threatened by these evil forces. They flatter us, tempt us, and try to dissuade us from giving priority to the kingdom of God. We have been told—and we have experienced in so many ways—that in our struggles to remain loyal to God and His agenda for our life, "we are not contending against flesh and blood, but against the principalities, against the powers, against the world rulers of this present darkness, against the spiritual hosts of wickedness in the heavenly places" (Ephesians 6:12). That's why the apostle Paul urges us not to take these demonic forces and the way they operate lightly, but to "be strong in the Lord and in the strength of his might" and to "put on the whole armor of God, that you may be able to stand against the wiles of the devil" (verses 10, 11).

Of course, D-day has dawned in this war too. The devil has already been defeated. His place is no longer found in heaven (Luke 10:18). His powers have been greatly curtailed. God, not this prince of darkness, is in control of our lives, time, and circumstances. Christ, the One who sends us on our mission of reconciliation, holds all authority, and He has given us " 'authority to tread upon serpents and scorpions, and over all the power of the enemy; and nothing shall hurt you' " (Luke 10:19; cf. Matthew 28:18–20). Consequently, when we pray with Christ the petition " 'thy will be done,' " we are expressing our desire that God make an end to all the powers of evil in us and around us so that His plan of salvation will be fully implemented " 'on earth as it is in heaven.' "

The *legalistic* misunderstanding

Just as we can hasten the coming of God's kingdom, so we can also hinder it from being fully realized. Jesus tells us that our entering the kingdom of God depends to a large extent on our doing the will of His Father who is in heaven (Matthew 7:21). A series of misunderstandings and misinterpretations exist regarding this and other statements in the New Testament regarding God's will.

First, there is the *legalistic* misunderstanding. It postulates that the Ten Commandments embody and express the will of God and that the full implementation of His will depends upon all people keeping them faithfully and in perfection.

Let's be clear about it: the Ten Commandments do, indeed, express the design for our living that God Himself has given us (Ecclesiastes 12:13). And if people more faithfully obeyed these commandments, our world would be a better place. We'd have fewer wars, stronger family lives, better relationships with our neighbors, etc.

In fact, Jesus Himself told us in the very same inaugural address in which He gave us the Lord's Prayer that He had not " 'come to abolish the law and the prophets; . . . but to fulfil them.' " And He added, " 'Truly, I say to you, till heaven and earth pass way, not an iota, not a dot, will pass from the law until all is accomplished. Whoever then relaxes one of the least of these commandments and teaches men so, shall be called least in the kingdom of heaven; but he who does them and teaches them shall be called great in the kingdom of heaven. For I tell you, unless your righteousness exceeds that of the scribes and Pharisees, you will never enter the kingdom of heaven' " (Matthew 5:17–20).

The Ten Commandments apply to all people for all time. In fact, keeping the law is a sign of our love to God and a hallmark of those ready to enter into the kingdom of God (John 14:15; 1 John 5:3; 2 John 6; Revelation 14:12). "The law is holy, and the commandment is holy and just and good" (Romans 7:12).

Where, then, lies the misunderstanding? In the conclusion that it is the keeping of the law alone that is evidence of doing God's will. It is not. Think, for instance, of the rich young ruler who had kept the commandments from his youth on. He was not ready to enter the kingdom of God, though he thought he was. In fact, he was far from doing the will of God (Luke 18:18–30). Compare his story to that of the cheating and deceiving tax collector who heard from Jesus' lips, " 'Today salvation has come to this house' " (Luke 19:9). Or Jesus' words to those who had prophesied in His name, cast out demons, and done many mighty works in His name: " ' "I never knew you; depart from me, you evildoers" ' " (Matthew 7:23).

The will of God as described in Scripture has two dimensions—two pillars, as it were—grace and obedience. The latter is not possible without the former. Grace comes first and is the basis of all obedience. Grace means unconditional love toward a person who doesn't deserve it. Grace is what is revealed by the verse, "While we were still helpless, . . . Christ died for the ungodly" (Romans 5:6, NASB). This love of Christ prepares and helps us to be obedient. Doing God's will is an act that God Himself works in us "for his good pleasure" (Philippians 2:13). It is He—God Himself—who will put His law within us and write it upon our hearts (Jeremiah 31:31–34). That law within us gives us a new way of thinking and acting. And if we make a mistake—and we all do—God is there to forgive us, and He covers us by His grace.

So it is by God's grace and not by our keeping the commandments that the will of God is fulfilled in us. The kingdom is realized in us, Jesus tells us, when we " 'repent, and believe in the gospel' " (Mark 1:14). As an expression of God's will, the commandments can teach us and berate us, instruct us and convict us. But it is grace that forgives us and restores us, inspires us and empowers us to do God's will. It is as we experience God's love for us that we are enabled and compelled to love—to love the Lord our God with all our hearts and with all our souls and with all our minds, and our neighbors as ourselves. " 'On these two commandments depend all the law and the prophets' " (Matthew 22:40). " 'If a man loves me,' " Jesus said, " 'he will keep my word, and my Father will love him, and we will come to him and make our home with him' " (John 14:23;

cf. verse 15). And thereby is the will of God accomplished. It is that simple and that profound. "Thy will be done" means "may Thy love be realized in us and in all people and bear much fruit."

The *fatalistic* misunderstanding

The second misunderstanding is a *fatalistic* one that through the ages has led many a believer to give up his or her trust in the heavenly Father. It says that everything that happens in our lives and that of others is the result of or an expression of the will of God: good things and bad; small things and big; war and peace; the Holocaust and Hurricane Katrina; the terrorist attack on the World Trade Center in New York City on September 11, 2001, and the stock market crash; the winning of a lottery and a mother's loss of her baby; a promotion at work; a special deal in buying a new house; and the death of a loved one through cancer.

Certainly, there are biblical statements that can be read as supporting this view. But such an interpretation doesn't fit the scriptural picture of God's agenda of love. It flies against the whole biblical notion of human freedom, the divine gift of our making our own decisions, whether for the right or the wrong. This freedom is an essential hallmark of our dignity as creatures made in the image and likeness of God. Without that freedom, God's love could elicit only an echo from us, not a real love in return. Without that freedom, God's light would find only reflectors, not new light bearers who are able to let our " 'light so shine before men, that they may see your good works and give glory to your Father who is in heaven' " (Matthew 5:16).

It is true that as a result of humanity's revolt against God, the image of God in humankind has been greatly distorted, but it hasn't been destroyed. Our relationship with God has been broken—but not broken off!

Over the centuries, churches have split and remain divided over the issue of how much of that image of God—that ability to make decisions in freedom—still remains. Some speak of humankind's total depravity and a resultant inability to make any decision, while others believe in humanity's freedom to choose or reject salvation. Even John Calvin suggested that in spite of humankind's depravity, some *"scintillae"*—some "sparks"—of freedom remain. Otherwise, we couldn't be held accountable for what we have done or left undone; we wouldn't be responsible, and therefore wouldn't fall under the judgment. It is a terrible misunderstanding to attribute everything that happens to us and to others to the will of God. The idea doesn't even offer comfort!

When I was a boy, a military fighter plane crashed on an elementary school in the city where I grew up, killing forty-two students and two teachers. At the funeral, the minister asserted, "God was at the controls." No, Reverend, He was not! The responsibility for this tragedy lay upon the young pilot, who had wanted to impress his fiancée, who lived a block from that school, with how long he could keep his plane in a steep dive.

God tells us clearly that He takes no pleasure in the death of anyone (Ezekiel 18:32). In other words, it isn't His will that anyone should die. It is unimaginable that a father—any father who loves his children—could cause their death. And God is our Father, and He is much more inclined and much more able to care for His little children and protect them than any earthly father (cf. Matthew 7:11)!

Why, then, all this pain and suffering, death and disease, war and crime? It is a terrible misunderstanding to blame God for it all. There is, on the one hand, our human ability to do good and evil, for which we ourselves are responsible and will be held accountable. " 'Out of the heart come evil thoughts, murder, adultery, fornication, theft, false witness, slander. These are what defile a man' " (Matthew 15:19, 20). On the other hand, nature itself—and our bodies are a part of nature—is still subject to futility, subject to its bondage of decay (Romans 8:18–25). And finally, though this explanation should be used with hesitancy and great care, demonic spirits surrounding us are doing their work of evil.

We would do well to keep in mind the word of the apostle Paul to the

Corinthians, "Do not pronounce judgment before the time, before the Lord comes, who will bring to light the things now hidden in darkness and will disclose the purpose of the heart" (1 Corinthians 4:5). We shouldn't comfort one another with " 'empty nothings' " (Job 21:34) but with the assurance that God is our Father, our Dad, who knows all things and understands all things, who cares for us, whose love never ends, and who is present wherever we are and in whatever condition we may find ourselves. Even if "our hearts condemn us," writes the apostle John in his first letter, "God is greater than our hearts, and he knows everything" (1 John 3:20). No impersonal DNA, destiny, fate, or astrological sign; no sickness, grief, anxiety, or distress, "nor anything else in all creation, will be able to separate us from the love of God in Christ Jesus our Lord" (Romans 8:39).

The Torangwa Tower of Babel story

The tribes of the Upper Tor River Basin understood the will similarly to the way the languages of Scripture do, as "good pleasure, desire, plan, agenda," or "purpose." So, our meditations on the Lord's Prayer easily turned to the question of how they saw the plan for their lives, the purpose for their fragile and marginal existence. Illiterates these people all were, without any written form of language, but also thinkers and philosophers! Here is how they saw the overall unifying theme and plan for their lives:

In the beginning, gods and humans all lived happily together in one place. Nobody got sick; nobody died. There was plenty of food for all. Then one day, Tworadja, the lord of the animals, came and said, "I have brought you more and better food that will make you all happier still—I have brought you pigs. However, when you go into the forest to kill them, you must return to me the heart and the liver. They are mine, for I am the lord of the animals. Great harm will follow if you do not recognize me as such."

When our ancestor killed his first pig, he opened it up and saw that the heart and the liver were good for food and a delight to the eyes . . . and to be desired [to use the words of Scripture; see Genesis 3:6]. He and his companions ate them and did not return them to the rightful owner of the animals.

When they returned to their village, everything had changed. The fruits were withering. People became ill and later died. The food that nature had offered them so plentifully disappeared. There was quarreling and fighting. Life became extremely harsh. And worst of all, the gods had disappeared from the village. They had moved up into the sky, which from that moment on was as far removed from the earth as it is now—an enormous abyss between us humans and our gods. People felt lonely without the gods, at a terrible loss in this wide, wide world, and very much afraid. So they decided to build a huge tower that would reach up into the sky. It would be a point of orientation for them and also a huge ladder that would restore contact and relationship with the gods.

This they did; they built a huge tower that reached up into the sky to restore the relationship with the gods. When they had reached a considerable height, the gods took the tower—which was full of the people who were working there and finding solace there—lifted it up high, and then dropped it. While it was falling, the gods called for a strong wind, which blew the people in every direction. Some landed right in their old village; others were blown east or west or north or south and landed in faraway places.

But we have not given up. We must continue to build our huge towers [the *kone,* their sacred temples] until the relationship with our gods has been restored. That's what we are living for and hoping for. And one day it is going to happen.

This sacred story from the people of the Tor—the *Torangwa,* as they called themselves—was the first Tower of Babel story ever discovered outside of the Bible other than the ziggurat story of ancient Babylon. Like the Bible story, this tale gives an explanation for the huge racial, cultural, and religious diversity among the peoples of the world.

This story opened up an effective point of contact for the gospel. I could assure the Torangwa that they need not any longer try to climb up to God. He has seen our sufferings and shown His compassion by coming down to us, His creatures. He became as one of us and has lived among us, forgiving us our sins, healing our sick, waking up the dead, and promising us life more abundant than ever before.

Jesus came in the form of a servant—a Person like we ourselves, suffering hunger and pain, loneliness and disappointment.

> He was despised and rejected by men;
>   a man of sorrows, and acquainted with grief. . . .
> He has borne our griefs
>   and carried our sorrows. . . .
> He was wounded for our transgressions,
>   he was bruised for our iniquities;
> upon him was the chastisement that made us whole,
>   and with his stripes we are healed (Isaiah 53:3–5).

This same Jesus has told us, " 'Let not your hearts be troubled; believe in God, believe also in me. In my Father's house are many rooms. . . . And when I go and prepare a place for you, I will come again and will take you to myself, that where I am you may be also' " (John 14:1–3). That is, in a nutshell, God's will for us.

What a liberation this was! What good news! There was no need anymore to reach out to the gods above and placate them or to beg them to come back. God Himself came down to us in the form of Jesus Christ to reconcile us to Himself, not counting our trespasses against us (2 Corinthians 5:16–21).

Like a candle, their pregospel agenda of life had given them some light in the dark and some warmth. But when the sun of the gospel arose, that same candle cast a shadow! They accepted God's plan for their life— His will, His agenda—and they are now praying, *"Surga desgeretsirem am tanenah djeemgerater."* ("May Your plan [will, purpose, agenda] be accomplished among us, as it is in Your place.")

How we can know God's will for us

God's will, then, embodies His plan of salvation. To that end, He gave us His own Son so that whoever believes in Him should not perish but have eternal life. To that end, He sent us His Spirit to comfort us and to counsel us, to instruct us and to lead us into all truth, to guide us and to keep us connected with our Father, to sanctify us and to have us bear the fruits characteristic of a citizen of the kingdom of God: love, joy, peace, patience, kindness, goodness, faithfulness, gentleness, and self-control (John 14:15–17; 16:7–11; Galatians 5:22).

Here lies the answer to the question of whether we can know the will of God for us, which includes the decisions we all have to make at times: whom to marry, whether we should move to another city to start a new job there, whether to have or adopt another child, whether to study medicine or prepare for the ministry, whether to work overtime or stay at home more. God is, indeed, concerned about our well-being (3 John 2). He cares greatly about each of us (1 Peter 5:7).

The two most important things we can do to know God's will for us personally are to stay connected with our heavenly Father through prayer and to allow the Spirit of God to work in our lives. Jesus used the example of a vine and its branches to describe our connectedness with God and the fruit-bearing that results. " 'Abide in me, and I in you. As the branch cannot bear fruit by itself, unless it abides in the vine, neither can you, unless you abide in me. I am the vine, you are the branches. He who abides in me, and I in him, he it is that bears much fruit, for apart from me you can do nothing' " (John 15:4, 5). The apostle Paul wrote similar counsel to the Romans: "I appeal to you therefore, brethren, by the mercies of God, to present your bodies as a living sacrifice, holy and acceptable to God, which is your spiritual worship. Do not be conformed to this world but be transformed by the renewal of your mind, that you may prove what is the will of God, what is good and acceptable and perfect" (Romans 12:1, 2).

Yes, it is possible to know the will of God for us personally—to know what is the right thing to do at a given moment, the right thing to say. Is not this what we also learn from the life of Christ? In addition to being God, He was a human being like we are—in everything made like other human beings (Philippians 2:5–7). Yet He knew exactly what God's will for Him was, and He acted accordingly.

What is it that stands out in Jesus that is so different from us and other human beings? Two things: He was totally committed to His Father and closely connected with Him, and He was fully dedicated to the well-being of others—bearing the fruits of the Spirit in all His thoughts and actions. The same two means by which Jesus knew the will of the Father for Him will work for us too. If we remain connected with God through prayer and the indwelling of His Spirit, we will bear the fruits of the Spirit. For that reason, too, we are urged to become "renewed in the spirit of [our] minds, and [to] put on the new nature, created after the likeness of God in true righteousness and holiness"; to have the mind of Christ (Ephesians 4:23, 24; Philippians 2:1–5).

Praying with Christ " 'Thy will be done,' " then challenges us to examine ourselves as to whether Jesus Christ is really in us (2 Corinthians 13:5). If we do so, we shall experience anew the peace, the joy, and the certainty of knowing God's will for us and for the whole world.

For Further Reflection

1. The core meaning of the petition "Thy will be done, / On earth as it is in heaven" refers to the implementation of God's plan of salvation. What does that imply?

2. In what way has God's will already been implemented in heaven—both in the aspects of peace, righteousness, and joy and in the aspect of God's absolute authority over all His creatures, including the evil one?

3. What is the role of the church and of individual believers in fulfilling God's plan of salvation "on earth as it is in heaven"? What kind of believers should we be in order for God to use us as His instruments of salvation?

4. In the Garden of Gethsemane, Jesus asked that He be released from carrying out God's plan of salvation, but then He continued to the bitter end, obeying God's will. What are some of the most difficult issues we face in being used as instruments in God's hand to do His will, to implement His plan of salvation?

5. What is meant by the "legalistic" and the "fatalistic" misunderstandings of doing the will of God? Can we humans know what God's will is for us individually?

GIVE US THIS DAY OUR DAILY BREAD

How striking, at first sight, are the differences between the fourth petition, "Give us this day our daily bread," and the three previous ones! The first three all deal with spiritual matters; this petition seems so material. The first three center on God, *His* holy name; *His* kingdom, and *His* will; this one focuses on our needs. The first three show concern for the whole world—the fate of nations and power structures and the fulfillment of God's mission in all the world; this one asks for a favor regarding an individual's existence. The first three point to the fulfillment of a future event—the near future, certainly—nevertheless the future; this one deals with the present, the here and now, the immediate.

Many interpreters of the Lord's Prayer, including many of the Church Fathers, have pointed also to the three petitions that follow, which ask for the forgiveness of our sins, the power to resist temptations, and deliverance from evil—in other words, spiritual things—and then have concluded that this petition for our daily bread refers to our "spiritual bread"—the bread that comes from heaven, bread that does not perish but that lasts forever. After all, Jesus told the crowd that came to see Him, " 'Do not labor for the food which perishes, but for the food which endures to eternal life' " (John 6:27). And when the people said in protest, " 'Our fathers ate the manna in the wilderness; as it is written, "He gave them bread from heaven to eat," ' " Jesus then said to them, " 'Truly, truly, I say to you, it was not Moses who gave you the bread from heaven; my Father gives you the true bread from heaven. For the bread of God is that which comes down from heaven, and gives life to the world.' . . . 'I am the bread of life; he who comes to me shall not hunger, and he who believes in me shall never thirst' " (verses 6:31–35). Indeed, happy the person who eats of this bread daily!

These same interpreters also argue that Jesus Himself told the crowd to whom He gave this special prayer,

> "Is not life more than food, and the body more than clothing? Look at the birds of the air: they neither sow nor reap nor gather into barns, and yet your heavenly Father feeds them. Are you not of more value than they? . . . And why are you anxious about clothing? Consider the lilies of the field, how they grow; they neither toil nor spin; yet I tell you, even Solomon in all his glory was not arrayed like one of these. But if God so clothes the grass of the field, . . . will he not much more clothe you? . . . Therefore, do not be anxious, saying, 'What shall we eat?' or 'What shall we drink?' or 'What shall we wear?' . . . your heavenly Father knows that you need them all" (Matthew 6:25–32).

In the minds of these interpreters, then, the petition "Give us this day our daily bread" means: Give us each day our *spiritual* food, food that comes from heaven; food that gives our life meaning and hope, courage and strength—food that relieves us of our daily stresses and anxieties, food that helps us cope with our daily worries and concerns and that reminds us every day that we do not live by bread alone " ' "but by every word that proceeds from the mouth of God" ' " (Matthew 4:4).

Our daily needs

Yet as biblical as these interpretations are—and we do well to follow them—there is another side to the story: God is, indeed, concerned about our daily bread in the material sense of that word. The bread Jesus taught us to pray for every day refers to what we need every day to continue to exist: the food we need for our nourishment, but also the money we need to buy it, and the work we must have to earn the money to buy the physical necessities of life.

Think of the many instances through the centuries in which God Himself provided His people with bread! Think of the prophetic description of the new earth, when God's kingdom will have been restored to its intended form, and there will be plenty of food for all:

> "Ho, every one who thirsts,
>   come to the waters;
> and he who has no money,
>   come, buy and eat!
> Come, buy wine and milk
>   without money and without price" (Isaiah 55:1).

And think of the many parables in which Jesus describes the realities of the kingdom of God in terms of eating and drinking, of dinner parties and food "fests."

How often Jesus explained His Father's care for His people in terms of literal bread! " 'What man of you, if his son asks him for bread, will give him a stone?' " (Matthew 7:9). Jesus fed the crowd because He had compassion on them, He changed water into wine to save the bridegroom from embarrassment, and He sent His disciples on their mission breadless so they would learn that God would provide for them (Mark 6:8).

Yes, our Father is very much concerned about our daily material needs. Actually, it is unthinkable that we—children of the heavenly Father—could talk to Him only about His holy name, the coming of His kingdom, the judgment, or the resurrection of the dead and not cry out to

Him when we feel hungry or thirsty! What kind of father would require that? We might even state that we can't have any of the so-called spiritual aspects of life and thought if we don't receive our daily bread. So, God is as concerned about our physical well-being as He is about our souls (3 John 2).

Moreover, the Bible doesn't follow our typical Western division of life into the so-called spiritual things on one hand and the material things on the other—with the former superior to the latter. Made from the dust of the earth, we humans aren't just spiritual beings; we are flesh—without any inferior connotation attached to that part of our nature. Jesus Himself became flesh, and the Bible speaks of a resurrection of the flesh—not as something inferior to the spirit but as a sign that the two belong together and constitute a single unit. We aren't some being broken into pieces with one part superior to the other. We constitute one whole being in which each part participates in the other. We worship God as a total unit: body, soul, and spirit. The apostle Paul writes that our *body* is a temple of the Holy Spirit (1 Corinthians 6:19). So, eating and drinking—the most basic physical acts supporting our existence—are acts of worship if done to the glory of God (1 Corinthians 10:31).

The Lord's Prayer also forms such a unit. In its spiritual and physical concerns, it doesn't consist of a superior and an inferior part, one that's heaven-oriented and the other earth-oriented. Even the most spiritual aspects of this prayer, such as the hallowing of God's name and the coming of His kingdom, are earth-oriented. They deal with our existence on earth now and in the future. Consequently, people have pointed out that this petition for our daily bread—found right in the middle of the Lord's Prayer, with three petitions before it and three petitions after it—should be considered the spiritual as well as the literal center of the prayer.

This prayer had a special significance for the disciples of Christ, who had given up everything to follow Him: their professions, their families, their homes, their time, and their ability to produce enough food for their daily existence. Upon one occasion, the apostle Peter reminded Jesus of this: " 'We have left our homes and followed you,' " he said, to which Jesus replied, " 'Truly, I say to you, there is no man who has left house or wife or brothers or parents or children, for the sake of the kingdom of God, who will not receive manifold more in this time, and in the age to come eternal life' " (Luke 18:28–30).

The Source of our life

In our prayer for daily bread—that is, for food and shelter and clothing—we recognize our total dependence upon God our Father. We recognize that without Him who created us, we wouldn't even be alive, be able to think or to act, to relate or to communicate. It is, indeed, as the apostle Paul said to the men of Athens—those philosophers and literary giants at the Areopagus—" ' "in him we live and move and have our being" ' " (Acts 17:28).

It is at this point that the prayer "Give us this day our daily bread" gains new significance in our time. By our science and technology, we have created our own world: we have made land out of oceans, produced new miracle crops, grown gardens in deserts, created animals in test tubes, and eradicated smallpox and a host of other diseases that in the past ravished our societies. It seems we humans hold the whole world in our hands! We depend on no one but ourselves. We even plan our own future—a new world order.

Because of all this, we—believers and unbelievers alike—stand in danger of forgetting how dependent we are on what God has made: the earth and its fertility; fresh water; the right mixture of oxygen, hydrogen, and nitrogen; the right amount of ozone; the right distance from the sun. Where would we be if suddenly these elements and conditions no longer existed? We're already concerned about global warming and the decline of clean air and safe food, to say nothing about our need for energy.

Once in a while, God in His mercy reminds us of our dependence upon Him by sending us droughts, earthquakes, tsunamis, rainstorms, and floods (2 Kings 8:1; Psalm 105:16; Jeremiah 24:9, 10). When we pray with Christ, " 'Give us this day our daily bread,' " we declare our total dependence on God and His creation for our everyday existence. Whether we will have enough food, clean water, and pure air depends on our heavenly Father. If He would withdraw from this earth, it would collapse—and all of life with it. We would die of famine or pollution, heat or cold. It is God who, in His grace,

> makest springs gush forth in the valleys; . . .
> they give drink to every beast of the field. . . .
> Thou dost cause the grass to grow for the cattle,
>   and plants for man to cultivate,
> that he may bring forth food from the earth,
>   and wine to gladden the heart of man,
> oil to make his face shine,
>   and bread to strengthen man's heart (Psalm 104:10, 11, 14, 15).

What would happen if God would turn away from this earth and abandon it to us?

> These all look to thee,
>   to give them their food in due season.
> When thou givest to them, they gather it up;
>   when thou openest thy hand, they are filled with good
>   things.
> When thou hidest thy face, they are dismayed;
>   when thou takest away their breath, they die (Psalm 104:27,
>   28).

Everything exists by God's grace. He keeps His creation in shape and keeps on renewing it by His Spirit so that we may have our daily bread. However, God's provision certainly doesn't mean that we needn't work to obtain what we need. We surely must—quite often in the sweat of our face (Genesis 3:17–19). Paul counseled the church, "If any one will not work, let him not eat" (2 Thessalonians 3:10). So, when we pray, "Give us this day our daily bread," we are actually petitioning God to create the conditions that will enable us to get that bread. Be it soil or sunshine, rain or rare minerals, clean water or fresh air—whatever is essential for the production of food comes as a gift from our Father in heaven. And it is through His generosity that the supply is sustained, even in the face of our extravagance, waste, and exploitation of the earth.

Praying, then, with Christ, " 'Give us this day our daily bread,' " is asking God to continue to preserve and protect His creation so that it may bring forth grains and fruits and all the good things we need for our life and existence—and for the health and the ability to work for it. At the same time, we also pledge to God that we will wholeheartedly involve ourselves in preserving His creation, protecting the environment He has given us, and helping people find meaningful work so that they can earn their bread. We cannot pray, "Father, create the right conditions on this earth so that we may find food for the day and shelter and clothing," while we are busy polluting the earth and destroying our environment!

To be shared

Jesus began His prayer with the plural personal pronoun *our,* teaching us to address God as " 'our Father.' " When we pray that phrase, we're saying that we recognize all those who pray to this same Father as our own brothers and sisters. All distinctions of race, class, age, gender, or nationality have lost their significance here. If they once did make a difference in our thinking and behavior, since we have accepted Christ and pray with Him and in His name, they do so no longer (2 Corinthians 5:16–19; Galatians 3:28).

In the petition for "our daily bread," this personal pronoun receives an added dimension. Here, the personal plural pronoun *our* means that every gift from God carries with it the intention that we share it with others. Think of God's grace, His great gift of salvation—we must share it with others; we have no choice. So it is with those special gifts of the Spirit too, such as faith and teaching and counseling, uttering wisdom and prophecies, healing and hospitality. They all are given "for the common good" (1 Corinthians 12:7). They are personal, but they belong to the community of faith. And think of those fruits that the Spirit gives us—love, peace, joy, kindness, and goodness. And those precious talents and abilities our heavenly Father bestows upon us: music, poetry, painting, and crafts. They all presuppose a relationship with others. So it is with *our* bread. It is given to us as *our bread,* and that's how we are to pray for it—we pray for *our* bread. It is given to us so that we may share it with others.

Who are these others with whom we must share our bread? We know the answer too well: those who, in spite of all their hard labor, are unable to make a living, to supply themselves and their loved ones with the most basic necessities of life, such as food and shelter, clothing and work—provisions to maintain their health and cope with the stresses of life. We aren't talking here about only those who live in regions ravished by famine or floods or earthquakes. The needs of those people are obvious, and we must share with them the bread we receive daily from our heavenly Father. But the needy are right with us and among us too. Those who have no work and no health insurance, those who can't cope with life's strains and stresses, the refugees and strangers in our midst. As the apostle James puts it, "What does it profit, my brethren, if a man says he has faith but has not works? Can his faith save him? If a brother or sister is ill-clad and in lack of daily food, and one of you says to them, 'Go in peace, be warmed and filled,' without giving them the things needed for the body, what does it profit? So faith by itself, if it has no works, is dead" (James 2:14–17).

All too long have we Christians prayed the Lord's Prayer without acting upon it, and prayer without any accompanying action is useless.

When we pray, "Hallowed be Thy name. Thy kingdom come," and "Thy will be done," are we not pleading with God to bring about those conditions that are the hallmarks of His holy name, His kingdom, and His will? Are we not praying for righteousness and justice, laws and structures that benefit all people equally and protect their value and dignity? And are we not pledging to work with Him to achieve this ideal? Is this too idealistic, as many have said and as most of us are suggesting by our inaction?

Anyone who prays to God must believe that God exists and that He rewards those who pray to Him (Hebrews 11:6). Jesus Himself taught us to pray, " 'Abba, Father, all things are possible to thee' " (Mark 14:36). When we pray, we should earnestly believe that " 'all things are possible with God' " (Mark 10:27). He will give the necessities of life to those who pray! It is our unconditional trust in our heavenly Father—our "Daddy"—that guarantees us a life in which all our necessities are fulfilled—like the ravens that neither sow nor reap, that have neither storehouse nor barn, yet are fed by God, and the lilies in the field that neither toil nor spin yet whose apparel not even Solomon in all his glory could match. Unconditional trust in God, our "Daddy," will never disappoint us or leave us empty-handed.

The early Christian church really lived this prayer. Scripture says,

They devoted themselves to the apostles' teaching and fellowship, to the breaking of bread and the prayers. . . . And all who believed were together and had all things in common; and they sold their possessions and goods and distributed them to all, as any had need. And day by day, attending the temple together and breaking bread in their homes, they partook of food with glad and generous hearts, praising God and having favor with all the people. And the Lord added to their number day by day those who were being saved (Acts 2:42–47).

That's how churches grow and the kingdom of God is established.

In reminding us how dependent on God we are for our needs, the Lord's Prayer also helps us understand in what way His blessings come. While Matthew has us pray, " 'Give us *this day* our daily bread,' " Luke teaches us to say, " 'Give us *each day* our daily bread' " (emphasis added). We would have overlooked this minor detail were it not for the fact that each expression carries its own message, or at least its own interpretation of one and the same message. The Greek word translated "daily" in both Luke's and Matthew's Gospels is *epiousios.* The problem is that we don't know what this word means. It occurs only here in the Lord's Prayer and nowhere else in Scripture nor anywhere in other Greek literature of that time. The word has been found on a papyrus from the fifth century after Christ that contains a woman's shopping list, but that use of the word hasn't helped us understand it any better.

Epiousios has been translated "essential, substantial, supernatural," and "supersubstantial," as well as "day-to-day," or even "the coming day's," and "tomorrow's." Many interpreters have chosen to translate it as "necessary." This petition, then, would read, "Give us this day our necessary bread," or "Give us today the bread that we need today." The meaning would be, "Give us as much as we need for our life and existence today—but not more than we need today."

This meaning is beautifully and powerfully illustrated by the experience of Israel on their journey through the desert, when God gave them each day their daily bread in the form of manna. Scripture says that the Israelites gathered "according to what [they] could eat," not more nor less. God supplied enough for the day. Everything that they gathered beyond what they needed for the day spoiled before the next day. Only on Friday could they gather a double portion, so they could keep the Sabbath holy, without the food spoiling (Exodus 16:14–30). When we pray for and receive only the bread we really need for each day, we won't forget our utter dependence on God's gift each and every day.

Receiving more than we need for each day could tempt us to forget

God and to lay up treasures on earth and put our trust in them. These riches would choke our interest in God and our dependence on Him (Matthew 6:19–21; 13:22). That's why Jesus told His disciples that it isn't easy for a rich person to enter into the kingdom of God (Luke 18:24–30). The Lord's Prayer helps us to realize that there is more to life than food and drink and clothing and houses and land and stocks and bonds. The life God intends us to live centers on His kingdom and its righteousness. If we live that way, then all these other things will be added (Matthew 6:31–33; Luke 12:29–31).

Give them to eat

The petition for our daily food and other essentials takes on a entirely different dimension when prayed in the setting of the Stone Age tribes that roam the dense tropical forests of New Guinea—tribes such as the Bora-Bora, the Berrik, the Daranto, and the Segar. When I worked among these marginal, seminomadic tribes, they all teetered on the brink of existence. In fact, a number of them, such as the Gooammar, the Soobar, the Ittik, and the Mander, have lost their battle for survival.

The natural environment had very little to offer the members of these tribes. They didn't plant or harvest, and they had no tools other than stone axes, the tusks of boars, and the teeth of rats with which to build their simple shelters and make the bows and the beautifully crafted and decorated arrows with which they fished and hunted. Every day they had to go out and gather whatever edibles they could find, which was very little. And every four to five years, when they had used up the resources around their village, they moved to another area in their territory, built a new village, and renewed the search for the food necessary for the day.

The staple food of these tribes was sago, which they prepared from the sago palm trees that grow in clusters scattered through the swampy areas in their territory. The men felled the palm trees, as they are the only ones who were allowed to touch their stone axes, which they acquired on long expeditions to the north. The women peeled away the bark, pounded the inside pith to a pulp, and rinsed it. Then they either mixed the pulp into baskets of hot water they prepared by heating stones in a fire and then dropping them into the water, or they wrapped the pulp in leaves and roasted it over open fires.

Other than the felling of the trees, the production of this staple food was totally in the hands of the women. The men of the tribe did go out every day *tjaree*—that is, "looking for food," in the hope of catching a fish or something, anything, that crept or crawled or flew. Once in a while, they killed a boar or caught little piglets to be raised by the women of the tribe. Most of the time, though, they returned from their hunts empty-handed, so they contributed very little or nothing to the daily food supply. This gave the women great power in those tribes. Not only were they the only ones who could give birth to the children whom the tribe needed for its growth and continuity, but they also were the primary ones upon whom the tribe depended for its sustenance. The men often said, of course, only when women weren't present, "How could we exist without our women?" In that society, the men were definitely the weaker sex, and they knew it. For that reason, tension between the sexes ran very high and often exploded in fights.

No society can exist without some kind of balance between the sexes. So, to counterbalance this "woman power," the men were the only ones who were allowed to enter the *kone,* the sacred house, and pray for fertility, growth, and food. They told the women, "You can work only on what we men let grow through our prayers." And the women, wisely, played along.

At first, then, when I began to teach the Bora-Bora to pray, the men insisted that women shouldn't be able to participate or even to hear the prayer. That was the men's prerogative, and theirs alone! They were afraid—and rightly so—that they would lose their status, and the balance of power would be broken. And that indeed happened, to the chagrin of the men. When women learned to pray, they told their husbands, "Who needs *you?*" The men responded in anger by beating the women. What was I to do? Exclude the women from hearing the good news of

God's kingdom and from praying the Lord's Prayer, as the men insisted? The situation grew worse before I found a solution.

To improve the people's ability to cope with life, I introduced steel axes. Then, what had previously taken a day or two and much sweat to accomplish took only an hour or two. The men could fell much bigger trees, so they could craft sturdier houses, bigger and better canoes, and larger and stronger rafts to negotiate the wild Tor and the other rivers—and all in much less time than had been required before. However, whereas the stone axes had been considered a gift of the gods because their origin was rooted in sacred mystery, there was no mystery about where the steel axes came from. That meant the women as well as the men could handle them, which robbed the men of their last vestige of power and status. They became very angry at me, and what might have been called progress was in fact a dismal failure—as many a Western do-gooder trying to help people in Africa and Asia has experienced!

The solution to the dilemma of status came when I introduced the men to laying out gardens, planting corn, and reaping the rich harvest. The soils in the Upper Tor River Basin were very fertile, and the hot climate was a help too. We harvested three crops a year. This gave the men enormous status, which was further enhanced by the fact that we had to move the domesticated pigs away from the villages because they continually disturbed and destroyed the plants. Keeping those pigs had been the role of the women, who now lost that part of their high status. Thus the balance was restored and peace began to prevail again—even to the point where men and women could pray together for the Lord to give them their daily food.

A central issue

The extreme scarcity of food in these primal populations of hunters and gatherers made food a central issue in all their thoughts and activities. To gain prestige or to humiliate their enemies, a tribe would prepare a feast and invite all the neighboring tribes to come and eat and sing and dance all night. Since the surrounding tribes were hungry most of the time, they felt compelled to accept those invitations, and they left these feasts feeling humiliated and defeated because of their own poverty. Once the Bora-Bora started growing corn, they had food aplenty and invited other tribes to many feasts. They were soon recognized, even in distant territories, as being the mightiest tribe in the area, and nobody dared to attack them any longer. They were considered to be the only super power.

Food was also at the core of all of these people's other human relationships. When strangers approached a village, the offer of food was a sign that they were welcome. The lack of such an offer meant, "Get out of here as quickly as you can. We can't guarantee your leaving this place alive." People who shared food together would address each other by a special term that means, literally, "we have eaten together." The relationship established by their sharing of food linked them to each other more closely than they were linked to their own brothers and sisters. In fact, sex was also tied to food in various ways. For instance, a woman who offered food to a man who wasn't her father, husband, son, or brother was considered to have committed adultery and was punished accordingly.

Among these tribespeople, every change of status was accompanied by ceremonies that centered in sharing food or in having to observe food taboos. When a woman was pregnant, her husband and brothers weren't allowed to eat pork. After a boy had been initiated into the tribe, he wasn't supposed to eat fish with scales until he had participated in another ceremony that made him a real man, ready to marry. The marriage ceremony itself consisted of the woman publicly offering her husband food, and he, in turn, putting food into her mouth. In effect, they were saying, "We have eaten together. Now, nobody and nothing can come between us or separate us from each other." And after death, food was at the core of the ceremony of the "burial of the bones." Everyone had to participate in this ceremony of eating together as a sign of solidarity; otherwise, they would be suspected of having been the cause of the deceased person's death.

One day while I was staying with the Nadjabaidja, another cannibalistic tribe from across the mountains—the much-feared and talked-about Moogit—attacked the village. They set the huts ablaze and tried to kill as many people as possible. We, of course, all fled. When the raid was over, I told the elders of the tribe how afraid I had been, to which they rather indignantly replied, "Why were you afraid? We have eaten together!" In other words, they were saying they would all have given their lives in my defense because "we have eaten together"!

So, as Jesus intended, the Bora-Bora considered eating in community the bread that God has given us to be an expression of hospitality and of solidarity with each other, of reconciliation, of having forgiven each other, of protection and care, of love and loyalty, and of the closest and deepest relationship that can exist between human beings. When they prayed, "Give us this day our daily food," they were asking for much more than sago alone. They were petitioning God for the ability to love their neighbor as themselves and to live in peace with everyone, to be kindhearted and to develop each day a closer relationship with their heavenly Father, who is the Giver of all the good things we need. And when they were baptized and participated in the Lord's Supper, they understood better than most of us the deep meaning of this ceremony that Christ Himself gave us.

The Bora-Bora also considered all bread received by any member of the tribe to be "our bread." When one hunter killed a boar, the whole tribe shared the meat. As long as one family had something to eat, we all had something to eat.

One day I came back from a hunt with a group of Bora-Bora men and discovered that all my boxes had been opened and everything in them had been taken: all my socks, shirts, pants, and underwear. Only my medicines and needles had remained untouched, out of fear. Triumphantly, the people showed me my socks, which they were wearing on their hands and arms. My shirts were being worn backwards, and they were using my underpants to cover their heads. How could they know how they were meant to be worn?

At first I wasn't amused. But the incident taught me the meaning of *our.* I was eating their food, sleeping in their huts, hunting and fishing with them. They had taught me how to walk across the rivers on trees they had felled to bridge them, and how to avoid attacks by boars. They had taught me their language and had accepted me as a brother, son, or father. So, my goods were "our goods"!

As the Bora-Bora tribe became stronger and more prosperous, their prayers for their daily necessities also became a corrective to one unintended consequence the change I had introduced brought with it. They had begun to enjoy the honor and high status they received when they shared the wealth of food that planting corn had brought them. In time, the gaining of power and prestige became a goal in itself—a means whereby they could dominate and control other tribes. Many of us then realized that this was an abuse of the precious gift of God, which He meant to remind us of our dependence upon Him and to share with others so that they, too, would honor Him. So we translated this chapter's clause of the Lord's Prayer as *"Dzjegeresse mere geeterbonne emmertaban,"* which means, "Give us today only what we need for ourselves and for sharing with others."

Bread that doesn't perish

Western churches have split over the issue of the meaning of Communion, and ecumenical discussions on participating in each other's celebration have ended in impasses. But these Stone Age people experienced the very essence of this precious sacrament in which people are made to realize that they truly have been reconciled to God and brought into a new fellowship of love with each other. They understood so much better than we do what the Jewish leaders' criticism of Jesus meant when they said on repeated occasions, " 'This man receives sinners and eats with them' " (Luke 15:2; cf. Matthew 9:11; Mark 2:16). To them, "God is eating with us, and we with each other" meant "We have been reconciled to God. Our sins have been forgiven. Nothing and nobody can separate us from the love of God. And nothing and nobody can estrange us: we are all brothers and sisters—one big family, with one God and Father of us all" (cf. 2 Corinthians 5:17–6:1).

The Lord's Prayer, in the context of the Sermon on the Mount in which it was given, challenges us to realize that in spite of all our wealth and prestige, our science and technology, our bakery shops and grocery stores, restaurants and farmers' markets, our air-conditioned homes and work opportunities and schools, our banks and natural resources, we are nothing and nobody were it not for God's gift of "our daily bread." Where would we be without the life and breath, fresh air and clean water, animals and plants, health and the abilities He gives us?

Even those of us who recognize God as our Creator and Sustainer tend to glorify our own achievements. We aren't immune to the satisfaction the Bora-Bora felt when they discovered the power and prestige wealth can buy. It shows up in the behavior and attitudes both of wealthy individuals and of wealthy nations that buy prestige and control with the aid they give to the poorer nations of the world. Even mission organizations and churches aren't immune to this attitude. It shows in our success mentality and in the pride of numbers and achievements, in our growth statistics and our often triumphant ways of reporting (cf. the sin of " 'number[ing] Israel,' " 2 Samuel 24). Not that God wants us to stop asking for His blessings or giving aid to others. To the contrary! And the more we ask for these daily necessities of ours and those of others, the more we shall receive. But the Lord's Prayer teaches us that we shouldn't use these divine gifts for our own power and prestige, honor and glory, but for God's!

Praying regularly for "our daily bread" may make us realize that advances in the kingdom of God aren't material goods or worldly honor or countable achievements, but a sense of humility and a poverty of the spirit, for the kingdom of heaven belongs to those who have these qualities (Matthew 5:3). Praying for our daily necessities starts and ends with the notion that we are really praying for Christ Himself, the true Bread of Life, to come into our hearts and stay with us (John 14:23).

For Further Reflection

1. Consider the differences between needs and wants. To what necessities of life does the petition for "our daily bread" refer?

2. How is the petition for "our daily bread" related to the biblical concept that "if any one will not work, let him not eat" (2 Thessalonians 3:10)?

3. Is the petition for "our daily bread" limited only to the poor and the unemployed—people who don't have the daily necessities of life? How does this petition apply to people who are rich, have good jobs, and possess nice homes?

4. God's gifts are always given with the intention that those who receive them share them with others. "My bread," "my work," and "my money," therefore, are given to us as "our bread," "our work," and "our money." Who besides us constitute the "our"? How could this be better implemented in our Christian communities? How did the early church understand and practice it?

5. Our divine Father is well aware of all our needs, and He wants us—His children—to prosper in every way (3 John 2). Why, then, does He want us to pray about our daily needs?

FORGIVE US OUR
DEBTS . . .

Social and behavioral scientists have made us very much aware of the fact that forgiveness is one of the most essential ingredients of a happy and fulfilled life, a life of peace, without anxieties and stress. No warm personal relationships are possible without it. We also have learned from physicians and nurses that patients' feelings of guilt, shame, and unforgiven debts strongly influence both the time and the nature of their healing. Hospice workers and chaplains, who accompany patients on the last phase of their life's journey, testify of the same. That's why many a religious ritual performed at the end stage of a person's life gives the dying person the opportunity to ask for and offer forgiveness. Happy the person, Scripture tells us, "whose transgression is forgiven, / whose sin is covered, . . . / to whom the LORD imputes no iniquity" (Psalm 32:1, 2).

What do we owe those from whom we ask forgiveness, God as well as our fellow human beings? In answering this question, it is important to consider the difference in wording in the Gospels of Matthew and Luke. Matthew teaches us to pray for the forgiveness of our " 'debts,' " while Luke speaks of the forgiveness of our " 'sins.' " Most likely, Matthew has given us the original version as spoken by Jesus Himself, as the Greek word Matthew uses here, *opheilemata,* is a literal translation of the Aramaic word *choba*, which means "debt."[1]

The term *debts* used in this passage originally referred to financial debts: loans and credits taken, wages that have not been paid yet (Romans 4:4), promissory notes, mortgages, things that were borrowed and not yet returned. Later, the term was also applied to anything people owed other people: parents who owe their children love, care, guidance, and protection; children who owe their parents honor, gratitude, and obedience (Exodus 20:12; Ephesians 6:1–4); employers who owe their employees a living wage; employees who owe their employers loyalty and work well done; other obligations of various kinds, such as citizens' obligations toward their government and vice versa; the obligations that stem from business and other contracts, such as marriage, landlord-renter contracts, etc. Above and beyond these, the term *debt* was also applied to obligations and expectations that can't so easily be defined, such as hospitality, friendliness, cheerfulness, loyalty, volunteerism, honesty, ethical behavior, diligence, and even the willingness to go the second mile.

In Jewish thinking at the time of Christ, the Aramaic term *choba* and its literal translation into Greek, *opheilemata,* implied that all of these obligations, duties, and expectations were considered a debt toward God, for in a life lived *coram Deo*—"before God"—love to God and to our neighbor implies that we fulfill them all. The term *debt,* then, implied a lack of love toward God and our fellow human beings, and therefore was considered sin—an act and sign of a broken relationship between God and us. In that sense, all people on earth have sinned and stand in need of forgiveness (Romans 3:23; 5:12).

Luke wrote his Gospel for the Greeks, who didn't consider financial,

---

1. In some communities of faith, people pray "forgive us our trespasses." The word *trespasses* doesn't appear in the Lord's Prayer in either Matthew or Luke. However, Jesus used the term in the explanation He gave of His prayer: " 'If you forgive men their trespasses, your heavenly Father also will forgive you; but if you do not forgive men their trespasses, neither will your Father forgive your trespasses' " (Matthew 6:14, 15).

social, and moral debts to be sin. To make clear to them what Christ really meant when He taught us to pray, Luke, therefore, rightly translates the term *choba* and its Greek equivalent as "sins," *hamartia*. He wanted his readers to understand that any unpaid debt or obligation, any unfulfilled promise or expectation, be it financial or social, ethical or moral, must be understood as a sin toward God.

These faults are indications that we haven't hallowed God's name as we should have, haven't worked with Christ for the arrival of God's kingdom, haven't allowed God to accomplish His will in us, haven't loved God and our neighbor with all our heart and soul and might—and that is called "sin." Had Luke translated the Aramaic word for *debt* literally, his Greek audience would never have grasped the depth of the term and would never have understood the true meaning of our prayer for forgiveness. However, once Luke had made that point, he could use the word *indebted* in the second part of the sentence (Luke 11:4).

What was true of Greek culture then, is equally true in many societies today. In modern Western cultures, even those rooted in Christian principles, people have lost the notion of sin and its consequences. We know of debts and obligations, but we refer to them as errors, shortcomings, failures, or mistakes, without any reference to God. And aside from those that bring legal consequences, these errors or mistakes bring few or no consequences—and few people recognize the need to ask forgiveness! But a prayer for forgiveness presupposes a conviction of wrongdoing, of a debt before God. Jesus said, " 'Those who are well have no need of a physician, but those who are sick' " (Matthew 9:12). It is this recognition and deeply felt sense of shame and guilt and indebtedness that leads us to pray, "Forgive us our debts."

All need forgiveness

To many Christians, sin is something substantial, like a stain on a bridal gown. One can see it, know it, touch it, sense it. It consists of deeds done against the express will of God or the neglect of things He specifically commanded to be done. In this sense, "sin is the transgression of the law" (1 John 3:4, KJV).

However, this definition implies that when people don't know the law, they aren't guilty of any transgression, for "where there is no law there is no transgression" (Romans 4:15). This notion of sin has led many believers to perfectionism because it suggests that people can keep the law satisfactorily simply by refraining from stealing, murdering, lying, or committing adultery. The rich young ruler thought this (Luke 18:18–27). It has also led to a rather superficial confession of our sins and has robbed many a believer of the deep joy and satisfaction of having our real sins forgiven and of entering a whole new relationship with God as our heavenly Father.

Sin has a much deeper dimension than merely this "substantial" one. It really consists of an attitude, a relationship, common to all people that lies at the core of our transgressions of the law. God originally created humankind in His own image. The core of that image consists of a relationship in which human beings recognize their total dependence upon God. The best way to define this relationship is "love," as in "God is love." This relationship defines our status and our innate dignity; our first ancestor, Adam, was therefore called the "son of God" (Luke 3:38).

For that love relationship to exist, it must be based upon freedom: the freedom to love God with all our might or not to love Him at all, and the freedom to accept our dependence upon Him or to go our way without Him. Without that freedom, our love is nothing but an echo, and our recognition of our dependence on Him resembles a tether.

Our first ancestors, however, abused that freedom, which was like a pot saying to the potter, "I don't need you" (Isaiah 64:8; Jeremiah 18:1–6). Our ancestors turned away from their Maker and followed their own agenda. We can't explain why they abused their freedom; there is no reasonable cause for what the Bible calls sin. But as a result of their turning away from our Creator, we are by nature bent. None of us naturally seeks God, tries to do good, or can of ourselves bring forth the fruits of the Spirit: love, joy, peace, patience, kindness, goodness, faithfulness, gentleness, and self-control (Galatians 5:22). We are still made in the image and likeness of God. It still defines our status and innate dignity. But that image is severely damaged. The relationship was broken, but not broken off.

So, in His infinite love, God decided to take upon Himself the punishment that justice required. To that end, Jesus came into this world so that whoever believes in Him need not perish, as the law demands, but can have eternal life (John 3:16). As Scripture tells us, "In Christ God was reconciling the world to himself, not counting their trespasses against them" (2 Corinthians 5:19). "He destined us in love to be his sons through Jesus Christ, according to the purpose of his will. . . . In him we have redemption through his blood, the forgiveness of our trespasses, according to the riches of his grace which he lavished upon us" (Ephesians 1:5–8; see also Philippians 2:6–11).

"The forgiveness of our trespasses." All we have to do now is to stand in awe and gratitude before this God, our heavenly Father, who paid such a huge price to restore us to His own image, "after the likeness of God in true righteousness and holiness" (Ephesians 4:24). It is in light of Christ's whole life on earth and of His cruel death on the cross that we see ourselves as we really are—sinners all, indebted to God forever, and in need of forgiveness. And it is through that forgiveness in Christ that we all have received the promise and the power to begin anew as sons and daughters of our heavenly Father, re-created into His image (Romans 8:16; 1 John 3:2).

If God has already forgiven our sins, why should we pray, "Forgive us our debts"? Does this petition refer to the total and final forgiveness that God has guaranteed at His final judgment, for which we daily thank Him and worship Him? Or does this prayer concern the debts we continue to incur every day as a result of our ongoing abuse of our God-given freedom?

The answer is both. We have, indeed, already received the promise of the forgiveness of our sins so that we won't come under judgment. In the words of John 3:18, " 'He who believes in him is not condemned' " (see also Acts 10:43; 13:38). However, like so many promises in Scripture, this promise, too, is conditional. We are called to "bear fruits that befit repentance" (Luke 3:8). Our forgiveness must show in our everyday life, in the way we act and think and treat others. We mustn't be like that servant of the king who received a full write-off for the millions he owed the king, but who failed to forgive the few pennies a fellow servant owed him. In the end, he lost the write-off and was put in prison (Matthew 18:23–35).

We also stand in need of God's daily forgiveness for not reaching the benchmark God Himself has set—that we love Him with all our minds and hearts and souls and our neighbors as ourselves. Despite the offer of God's grace and His call for us to live in total dependence upon Him, none of us lives up to this standard. But, thank God, His forgiveness is always new and more than sufficient for those who penitently ask Him for it (Psalms 86:5; 103:3; Isaiah 55:7; Jeremiah 33:8). There is nothing temporary or delayed about this forgiveness. We can experience it just as did that tax collector, who " 'went down to his house justified' " (Luke 18:14).

" 'As we . . . have forgiven' "

Many of God's promises are indeed conditional. Are they, then, ever dependent upon our actions? Of course not! Yet, at first glance, this seems to be the message contained both in this petition and in the explanation Jesus gave. Let's look at the text:

> "Forgive us our debts,
>> *As we also have forgiven our debtors.* . . .

> "If you forgive men their trespasses, your heavenly Father also will forgive you; but if you do not forgive men their trespasses, neither

will your Father forgive your trespasses" (Matthew 6:12–15; emphasis added).

The petition reads, "as we also *have forgiven* our debtors" (emphasis supplied). It is an act already completed, and it is on that basis, or so it seems, that we ask God to forgive us. Luke quoted Jesus as saying, " 'Forgive us our sins, *for* we ourselves forgive every one who is indebted to us' " (Luke 11:4; emphasis added). He seems to be arguing even more strongly than Matthew that it is our own act of forgiving—and that on a continuous basis—that is the condition upon which we're requesting God to forgive us. In His sermon on the mount, Jesus told the crowd, " 'The measure you give will be the measure you get' " (Matthew 7:2). Is His prayer an application of these words?

If our love and compassion were to be compared to God's, " 'then who can be saved?' " (Luke 18:26). Therein lies the first answer to the question of whether God's forgiveness depends on ours; there is no comparison between our love and God's love, between our compassion and God's grace. God *is* love; He *is* grace and compassion and forgiveness. What is implied here is what Jesus on many other occasions told us—namely, that when we pray, worship God, bring our offerings, or make a sacrifice of some sort, we should do so with the right attitude.

"If you are offering your gift at the altar, and there remember that your brother has something against you, leave your gift there before the altar and go; first be reconciled to your brother, and then come and offer your gift" (Matthew 5:23, 24).

"Why do you not judge for yourselves what is right? As you go with your accuser before the magistrate, make an effort to settle with him on the way, lest he drag you to the judge, and the judge hand you over to the officer, and the officer put you in prison. I tell you, you will never get out till you have paid the very last copper" (Luke 12:57–59).

Compare also that prayer of the self-righteous Pharisee (Luke 18:9–14) and another statement Jesus made about prayer: " 'When you pray, you must not be like the hypocrites' " (Matthew 6:5). " 'Beware of practicing your piety before men . . . for then you will have no reward from your Father' " (verse 1). It is our attitude that counts, and in particular our attitude—our willingness and readiness—to forgive others without asking how many times we should forgive them. As Jesus told Peter, Not " 'as many as seven times' . . . 'but seventy times seven' " (Matthew 18:21, 22).

A second answer to the question about whether God conditions His forgiveness of us upon our willingness to forgive others comes from that well-known parable Jesus told about the unmerciful servant: " 'The kingdom of heaven may be compared to a king who wished to settle accounts with his servants. When he began the reckoning, one was brought to him who owed him ten thousand talents.' " In current terms, a talent is worth about fifty thousand dollars, so the servant's debt amounted to about five hundred million dollars!

> "And as he could not pay, his lord ordered him to be sold, with his wife and children and all that he had, and payment to be made. So the servant fell on his knees, imploring him, 'Lord, have patience with me, and I will pay you everything.' And out of pity for him the lord of that servant released him and forgave him the debt. But that same servant, as he went out, came upon one of his fellow servants who owed him a hundred denarii."

A denarius was an ordinary day laborer's daily wage, at the time worth about ten cents. In other words, in current terms, he owed ten dollars.

"And seizing him by the throat he said, 'Pay what you owe.' So his fellow servant fell down and besought him, 'Have patience with me, and I will pay you.' He refused and went and put him in prison till he should pay the debt. When his fellow servants saw what had taken place, they were greatly distressed, and they went and reported to their lord all that had taken place. Then his lord summoned him and said to him, 'You wicked servant! I forgave you all that debt because you besought me; and should not you have had mercy on your fellow servant, as I had mercy on you?' And in anger his lord delivered him to the jailers, till he should pay all his debt. So also my heavenly Father will do to every one of you, if you do not forgive your brother from your heart" (Matthew 18:23–35).

The forgiveness we all have received in such great measure, and continue to receive day in and day out, must bear fruit in us (Luke 3:8). In receiving God's forgiveness, we ourselves become forgivers of others—though, of course, our forgiveness in no way matches His. When we recognize how God has loved us, we are enabled to love others, even our enemies and those who persecute us (Matthew 5:44). All those who experience God's forgiveness, even in the smallest measure, develop the attitude that enables them to forgive others. Our willingness to forgive, then, is in fact a reaction to the forgiveness we have experienced in Christ. It comes as a response to God's love, God's grace, and God's forgiveness. And as long as we hold on to this mind-set, this attitude, in spite of ongoing failures, we retain God's forgiveness and don't fall under judgment.

All those who have experienced this grace in their lives cannot but share it with those who go about troubled, unforgiven, full of fears and anxieties, stressed out, and in need of the message contained in the Lord's Prayer. As Paul said, "Put on then, as God's chosen ones, holy and beloved, compassion, kindness, lowliness, meekness, and patience, forbearing one another and, . . . forgiving each other; as the Lord has forgiven you, so you also must forgive" (Colossians 3:12, 13).

A one-way street

At the core of a Christian's thinking and behavior, relationships and communication is the notion of grace. Grace is unconditional love toward a person who doesn't deserve it. It is rooted in the character and being of God Himself, whose very essence is grace. It is bestowed upon all people unmerited and undeserved—out of love and not in response to what humans have done or thought. It is a one-way street, and it is free. It can be summoned up in the life, work, death, and resurrection of our Lord Jesus Christ. In Him, God's grace was effected, which we experience in the forgiveness of our sins and in our being made over again, into new beings created after the likeness of Jesus Christ Himself (John 1:17; Romans 3:19–31; Galatians 2:11–21; Ephesians 2:8, 9).

True, we don't fully live up to this value. If we did, we would live in a social order based on the constitution Christ gave us in His sermon on the mount instead of the social orders we still live in today, be they of a democratic capitalist nature or of a socialist flavor or a combination of the two. However, many individual Christians do strive toward organizing their thoughts and life in harmony with this core Christian value—grace.

This whole notion, however, flew in the face of another core value of the seminomadic, Stone Age people of New Guinea. That value is called *mooytabernawar*—"reciprocity." It says that every gift, every service offered, every kind or evil act committed creates an obligation, a duty on the part of the receiver to repay it. This system was a cultural response to the extremely harsh circumstances in which these people found themselves.

How did this value work? What did it mean in practical life?

Children were forever obligated to their parents for giving them life. As long as they lived, therefore, children must obey their parents, respect them, and take care of them. And a man who married a woman was thereby obligated to the woman's kin group. Marriage involved an exchange: the bridegroom and the group to which he belonged must compensate the family of the bride with another woman, commonly a sister or a "cousin." This practice is understandable since women are the only ones who can bear children, and they also were the only ones who produced the food necessary for the sustenance of the tribe. Thus, losing a woman to another family unit represented an enormous loss, which could be compensated only by receiving another woman in exchange.

Of course, in reality, the system didn't work smoothly. Many a bridegroom didn't have a sister or a cousin. And complications arose when the woman to be given in exchange for her brother's wife didn't want to go or didn't like the man she was to marry. In that case, the bride's group would then accept other gifts instead: pigs, special shells, bows and arrows, sacred flutes (considered life-givers there), and, a host of menial services that never ended. For instance, when a bride-giver group organized one of their competitive feasts, the bride-receiver's group was under obligation to cut the firewood, produce the food, carry the water from the river, etc. These obligations and duties were passed from generation to generation, which made everyone in the tribe in one way or another obligated and indebted to everyone else.

Once I distributed thirty brightly colored baseball caps that a trading company had given to me: red ones and yellow ones, blue ones and green ones, each with the name of the product they were advertising. People wore them with pride, and they made an interesting picture—naked people wearing colorful baseball caps!

After a day or two, it became obvious that the people to whom I had given caps either didn't have them anymore or were wearing different ones from those they had originally received. People to whom the owners of the caps were indebted had required them to hand the caps over. The caps made visible the debts various people owed.

A person or a group suspected of an evil act like stealing, adultery, or sorcery, that was thought to have caused sickness or death, could make amends only by offering in exchange something of equal value. For instance, a family suspected of having caused the death of a child had to give a child in exchange before peace could be restored between the families. The person accused of having committed adultery had to give another woman to rectify the wrong.

One day, a group of men from the Daranto tribe killed a pig while passing through Bora-Bora territory. When they didn't give half of the pig to the Bora-Bora on whose territory they had killed it, as jungle law required, the Bora-Bora responded by invading the Darantos' territory and abducting two young girls, who later would be given in marriage to Bora-Bora men. Other tribes thought this was the right thing to do: an eye for an eye; a tooth for a tooth; two girls for half a pig, including payment for punishment.

This value of reciprocity also shaped people's relationship with their gods. They said, "Our gods have given us the sago and the pigs. Now we owe them." They paid their obligations faithfully in the form of sacrifices, acts of worship, and strict adherence to the rules and taboos that had come with these gifts.

The religion of these people worked the other way too. They would honor their gods by organizing big food festivals for which they killed large numbers of their domesticated pigs in a ritualistic way, prepared plenty of sago, and even fasted so they would have as much food as possible to offer to the gods and to the many people from the surrounding tribes whom they invited to participate in these sacred rituals, which often lasted a week to ten days. After the feasts, the people would say, "Now our gods owe us."

When I brought up the notion of forgiveness, of the cancellation of our indebtedness and the release from our obligations, the tribespeople laughed. "That would lead to utter chaos," Oshemanyah, one of the wise elders, said. In their opinion, the notion that a god would offer us anything without expecting something in return was totally absurd. Their vocabulary had no word for *forgiveness,* and they had no concept of grace. Every word of theirs meaning "favor" or "act of kindness" or "gift"—all translations of the Greek New Testament word *charis,* which usually is translated "grace"—carried with it the notion of reciprocity. I wondered how I could ever convey to them the message that the God we serve forgives us all our debts and misdeeds freely because of the love and grace provided in His Son Jesus Christ, that God does so without compensating merit or good deeds on our part, and that grace is a one-way street— we don't deserve it, and we can't earn it. God gives it only because He is love; He is gracious.

Love trumps everything

Two events in the life of the Bora-Bora people gave concrete illustrations on which I could build for them a whole new understanding of grace. The first was Ewwan and Waiyin's marriage. Ewwan and Waiyin had grown up in the same village. The two became inseparable, and neither of them would associate with anyone else of the opposite sex. When Ewwan accompanied me on journeys to the various tribes of the Tor territory and beyond—which he did many times—he fasted and refused to spend anything on himself and saved every gift he received just so he could bring gifts to Waiyin. He loved her, and she loved him; and all the tribespeople knew about the deep love these two felt for each other.

One day, Ewwan made it known that he wanted to marry Waiyin. That raised the issue of the bride price. Ewwan was an orphan; the Bora-Bora tribesmen had found him somewhere in the jungle and brought him to their village. So he had no family—no sister or cousin to offer. And Ewwan owned nothing; he had no pigs or other items of value to offer. And he couldn't even offer the services of his family in exchange. That posed a problem. If he paid the bride's family nothing, there would be "chaos," in the words of the wise man Oshemanya.

But the couple did get married. The morning of their wedding day, Waiyin prepared the sago, and in the presence of everyone put some into Ewwan's mouth, and he put some in hers. Then people cracked jokes about the lovely couple, all couched in food terms. And everyone seemed happy.

Afterward, I asked Oshemanya privately about the issue of exchange, of *mooytabernawar*. He said, "In the case of true love, nothing else is needed." The Bora-Bora preferred the exchange marriage. But they have a form of marriage as well called "love marriage." When everyone is convinced that a man and woman really love each other, all requirements for exchange of a woman or wealth and other obligations are ignored—done away with. The laws and regulations given to prevent chaos aren't declared null and void, but they are trumped by love. However, it must be love indeed.

In his letters to the Romans and Galatians, the apostle Paul wrote some powerful passages—passages that the apostle Peter said contained "some things . . . hard to understand, which the ignorant and unstable [lawless men] twist to their own destruction" (2 Peter 3:15–17). Suddenly, those passages became very clear before the eyes of those Stone Age people. Love trumps the law that God gave us for our own protection. It forgives us our trespasses and releases us from our guilt and shame. It makes the law that is holy and righteous and good of no value as a means of salvation, as a means of entering a new life with Christ as our Groom. By God's loving-kindness, we are no longer under the law, and where there is no law, there is no sin. *"Azgemmes wayakentenah angtaneh, nensa dzjeemgemmes wayakentenah,"* the people now pray. ("Through Your loving-kindness do away with our obligations and debts.")

The second event that made clear the meaning of forgiveness occurred when a group of Bora-Bora tribesmen and I—by then an adopted son of the tribe—trekked on foot from the mighty Mamberamo River across the Gauttier Mountains back to our tribal territory. None of us knew the area we were crossing. As far as my guides were concerned, it was terra incognita. No tribes were known to live in the area. Maps from the government, based on air reconnaissance, showed no forms of habitation.

The trip, a seven- to ten-day journey on foot, was more difficult than we first anticipated. We had to carry all our food supplies and other necessities. The mountain ranges ran north and south and we were traveling west to east, which meant we had to cross them. Given the difficult terrain and daily temperatures in the nineties (Fahrenheit), compounded by humidity also in the nineties, all of us were soon close to exhaustion.

On the third day, we made bivouac early. As the men were preparing a small hut, they discovered footprints all over the place. By late evening, we realized that we were surrounded by unknown tribesmen. We put up guards, built some fires that we kept burning all night, and prayed. But just before daybreak the next morning, arrows came flying into our camp.

At first, we couldn't see anyone. Even in these mountains, the jungle is rather dense. Then, a battle erupted. The Bora-Bora tribesmen insisted that I stay in the small hut they had built the night before and pray. And that I did! And in these most difficult circumstances in which we all were facing death, God answered. He brought to my remembrance some words I had heard many years earlier when faced with a similar situation a few hundred miles farther east. In desperation, I left the little hut and shouted, *"Essaow, essaow; ammoy, essaow!"*

The fighting stopped. With their bows and arrows at the ready, the attackers cautiously came into our camp. They were tall warriors with painted faces, dressed in war gear, and wearing yellow flowers in their hair as a sign that they were going to kill. And our greetings were short and to the point: *"Essaow, essaow; ammoy, essaow!"* ("You are my friend; you are my brother!")

Adopted

The war leader of this tribe, Ewweren, took me by the hand and guided us through their large territory to their main village. There was food aplenty. At night we, the people of the Tor, stayed close together and kept our fires burning. But there was no need for our suspicion and precautions since we had all eaten together.

In the days and weeks that followed, we told each other who we were and where we came from. The members of this tribe told us their expectations of a cataclysmic event that would soon destroy the world. They had made preparations for this imminent trauma: they had built special huts and provided food for the dead ancestors they expected to return. They had also built barnlike houses to store the goods and valuables—*kago*—that they expected their ancestors to bring with them. And they spent many a day and night singing new songs and dancing new dances with which to greet them.

They asked me what I knew about the end of the world and the return of the "Ancestor." My narrative of the return of Christ and the events that accompany His coming fascinated them (Matthew 24; Luke 21). And when it came to what I expected Jesus to bring with Him at His coming, I emphasized the things that don't perish, such as the end of wars and killings, disease and death, and a new reign of love and justice, rather than the goods they were craving. But I assured them that with that reign of God also come all the things we humans need—food and shelter, clothing and precious valuables, besides fellowship and a new sense of community.

After three weeks, my Bora-Bora people and I were more than ready to go home. However, war leader Ewweren, who in the meantime had adopted me as his son, refused to let us go. He wanted us to stay and experience with his tribe the earthquake and huge flood that would open the earth and bring back the ancestors. But we had to go, and so we began to make our way home.

As I was about to climb the mountain range that bordered their valley on the east, Ewweren rushed up to us, shouting, "You are not going to leave! I am your father, and I told you not to go!" He was dressed for war, carrying a dagger made from a man's bone and wearing a yellow flower in his hair. Some of his tribesmen tried to stop him, to no avail. He was intent on killing me, the son who had the temerity of defying him, the father. "What would happen to our community if we allowed sons to disobey their own fathers?" these tribespeople had often instructed me before. "Utter chaos would be the result." And they had told me many stories about fathers who had indeed killed their own sons because of their disobedience. Now I was in that situation.

Disappointed, angry, and deeply hurt, Ewweren stood before me, dagger raised high. I was pleading with him, trying to make him understand my action. But he bristled. "You are my son," he said. "You are disobeying me. I must kill you." Then, suddenly, he lowered the dagger and looked around until he found his own son. Grabbing the young boy roughly by his hair, he threw him at my feet, and shouted, "Take him with you. He is no longer my son. I cannot kill you; I love you too much. Here's my son. Make a man out of him like you are. He is dead to me." Then he rushed away.

Instead of killing me for having disobeyed my own father, as the law of the tribe required, he gave me his own son and made him dead to himself. This experience opened the eyes of the Bora-Bora people to the meaning of the death of Christ. Through Him, we all have received forgiveness of our debts and sins—all because God loves us. And His love encompasses all people and endures forever!

Lost and found

Perhaps no parable of Jesus tells the story of God's forgiveness more powerfully, more beautifully, and more invitingly than the parable of the prodigal son.

"A man . . . had two sons; and the younger of them said to his father, 'Father, give me the share of property that falls to me.' And he divided his living between them. Not many days later, the younger son gathered all he had and took his journey into a far country, and there he squandered his property in loose living. And when he had spent everything, a great famine arose in that country, and he began to be in want. So he went and joined himself to one of the citizens of that country, who sent him into his fields to feed swine. And he would gladly have fed on the pods that the swine ate; and no one gave him anything. But when he came to himself he said, 'How many of my father's hired servants have bread enough and to spare, but I perish here with hunger! I will arise and go to my father, and I will say to him, "Father, I have sinned against heaven and before you; I am no longer worthy to be called your son; treat me as one of your hired servants."' And he arose and came to his father. But while he was yet at a distance, his father saw him and had compassion, and ran and embraced him and kissed him. And the son said to him, 'Father, I have sinned against heaven and before you; I am no longer worthy to be called your son.' But the father said to his servants, 'Bring quickly the best robe, and put it on him; and put a ring on his hand, and shoes on his feet; and bring the fatted calf and kill it, and let us eat and make merry; for this my son was dead, and is alive again; he was lost, and is found.' And they began to make merry" (Luke 15:11–24).

For Further Reflection

1. What are the "debts" for which we must ask forgiveness? Consider, in this regard, the differences between the sins of omission and those of commission and between "substantial" sins and "relational" sins—between acts of sin and wrong attitudes and broken relationships.

2. Why does Jesus teach His disciples and followers today, whose sins have already been forgiven through His death on the cross, to continue to pray for the forgiveness of " 'our sins' "? What sins does Jesus have in mind here: those that involve our standing before God when we appear before His judgment seat, or the sins of omission and commission that accumulate in our daily life?

3. Is God's forgiveness absolute, or is it tied to certain preconditions on our part? Is forgiveness something imputed to us outside of our will and activities, or is it bound by human actions and states of mind?

4. Forgiveness often comes at a great price. God Himself paid the ultimate price through the death of His Son to make the forgiveness of our sins possible. What difficulties—even sacrifices—do people often face when it comes to forgiving others? What blessings does God have in store for those who make those sacrifices and forgive others?

5. When forgiveness has been given, are the acts and issues that necessitated it forgotten, wiped out, done away with as if they had never happened?

LEAD US NOT INTO TEMPTATION . . .

Throughout the history of Christianity, people have pondered the true meaning of this sixth petition of the Lord's Prayer, " 'Lead us not into temptation, / But deliver us from evil.' " Questions have arisen over the meaning of the word *temptation* and especially over temptation's role in the life of the Christian. Is it God who tempts people or the devil or evil itself? And does it accomplish good or evil, something positive or something negative?

In our everyday understanding of *temptation,* the term means "an inducement to do evil, an allurement, an enticement toward something that may be enjoyable but that detracts from our true calling or character." Generally, we regard it as something negative. The term carries that sense in Scripture too—for instance, in Luke 4:2, 13, which speaks of Jesus Himself being tempted to lose sight of His calling and mission, and in James 1:13, 14, "Let no one say when he is tempted, 'I am tempted by God'; for God cannot be tempted with evil and he himself tempts no one; but each person is tempted when he is lured and enticed by his own desire." So, Jesus counsels us strongly, " 'Watch and pray that you may not enter into temptation' " (Mark 14:38).

But in Scripture, the term has a much wider connotation and a deeper meaning than just the inducement to do evil. At times, it even has a rather positive one. It can refer to the testing of a person—trying or proving that person, such as in Psalm 26:2, "Prove me, O Lord, and try me; / test my heart and my mind." Here, the psalmist calls upon God to test him in order to improve his character, to build him in the faith, to lead him into a closer walk with God. The Lord tested Abraham and Job in that way, and the Spirit led Jesus into the wilderness to be tempted by the devil (Genesis 22; Matthew 4:1–25). This "temptation," or testing, is for the person's own good, to establish the certainty of his or her salvation. In the words of the apostle James, "Blessed is the man who endures trial, for when he has stood the test he will receive the crown of life which God has promised to those who love him" (1:12).

This raises the question again of what Jesus had in mind when He taught us to pray, " 'Lead us not into temptation, / But deliver us from evil.' " The petition clearly consists of two interconnected parts: in the first, the petitioner asks to be led away from rather than into temptation, while the second part clearly indicates what kind of temptation Jesus was referring to—namely, that which leads to destruction, to giving up one's faith, to losing sight of one's high calling and destiny under God. That's the work of the evil one, from which power the person who is praying this petition seeks to be delivered.

So, the two parts of this petition form a unit in which we plead with our heavenly Father to lead us away from the kind of temptation that results in people giving up their faith, losing sight of their calling before God as citizens of His kingdom. For no believer can ever in his or her own strength keep the faith and remain loyal to God when tempted by the devil. "Let any one who thinks that he stands take heed lest he fall. No temptation has overtaken you that is not common to man. God is faithful, and he will not let you be tempted beyond your strength, but with the temptation will also provide the way of escape, that you may be able to endure it" (1 Corinthians 10:12, 13). It's not so much that we are praying for God, our Daddy, to keep temptations away from us, as temptations are inevitable as long as we live in this world. Instead, we are asking

Him for strength not to succumb to those temptations. Jesus asked His Father for the same thing for us: "I pray not that thou shouldest take them out of the world, but that thou shouldest keep them from the evil [one]" (John 17:15, KJV).

So, the petition reads, "Abba, Father, we are not asking You to keep us from temptation, but to help us to overcome it." And the good news is that God hears our prayers and empowers us to overcome any temptation that stems from the enticement of our own desires, as well as from the wiles of the evil one (James 1:14, 15; Ephesians 6:10–18).

The hour of temptation

Jesus pointed out that shortly before His return to this earth in all His glory, all people then living will face an immense trial such as never has happened before and never will happen again. False christs and false prophets will arise and show signs and wonders so deceptive and so enticing as to lead astray, if it were possible, the very elect (Matthew 24:1–31; Mark 13:14–22). As a result of this time of testing, the love of many will grow cold, and many will give up the faith altogether. Jesus wondered aloud, " 'When the Son of man comes, will he find faith on earth?' " (Luke 18:8). He knows that if He doesn't shorten the days of that trial, no human beings will be saved. But for the sake of the elect whom He has chosen, He will cut it short (Mark 13:20). We have Jesus' own word that He Himself will deliver us from that worldwide hour of temptation (Revelation 3:10), and we have God's great promise that He will never fail us nor forsake us (Hebrews 13:5; Deuteronomy 31:6).

Was this time of trouble the temptation Jesus had in mind when He taught us to pray, "Abba, Father, we don't ask You to keep us from this temptation but to help us to remain steadfast in the faith and loyal to our calling as Your sons and daughters"? Yes, indeed. And we may take His promise seriously that in that great hour of temptation, He will deliver us from the evil of giving up the faith and losing our redemption.

But was this the only temptation Jesus had in mind when He taught us to pray " 'lead us not into temptation' "? No. Jesus saw clearly that we are constantly beleaguered by temptations both from within and from outside of ourselves, and therefore we need to ask God daily to help us to overcome them, just as we pray every day for our daily bread. The hour of temptation is not just at the end of time. It is now. Now is the time when "the devil prowls around like a roaring lion, seeking some one to devour" (1 Peter 5:8). Now is the hour when we need "the whole armor of God, that you may be able to stand against the wiles of the devil. For we are not contending against flesh and blood, but against the principalities, against the powers, against the world rulers of this present darkness, against the spiritual hosts of wickedness in the heavenly places" (Ephesians 6:11, 12).

The devil knows that his time is short, for " 'now the salvation and the power and the kingdom of our God and the authority of his Christ have come' " (Revelation 12:10, see also verses 11, 12). He knows it, and so do we! God's kingdom has already been established! And as His children, we know that our heavenly Father has all power in heaven and on earth to protect us and to guide us, to lead us and to help us overcome any form of temptation the devil may throw at us. With Jesus we may say, " 'Begone, Satan! for it is written, "You shall worship the Lord your God / and him only shall you serve" ' " (Matthew 4:10). Scripture tells us that when Jesus said that, "the devil left him, and behold, angels came and ministered to him" (verse 11).

The temptation Jesus faced was similar to the one that Adam faced and that we still face: the temptation not to acknowledge God as our Father on whom we depend for life, health, strength, and ability; the temptation to live a life without God—a life in which we seek our own honor and status, glory and celebrity, all the while depending only on our own strength and talents; a life in which we speak of our self-realization instead of the realization of the principles of the kingdom of God.

Above and beyond all satanic powers in the world, both in us and outside of us, is the authority of our heavenly Father, who loves His children and who doesn't want any of them to be lost (2 Peter 3:9). Everything is under our Father's control—even the power of the devil. And we have God's own promise that He cares for us more than any earthly father ever could care for his children (1 Peter 5:7).

Deliver us from evil

Many interpreters have considered this petition asking God to deliver us from evil as a seventh petition, separate from the one that asks God not to lead us into temptation. That way, at least in Matthew's version, the Lord's Prayer consists of seven petitions. (Luke's version of the Lord's Prayer doesn't contain this petition.) Matthew wrote his version of this prayer for those Jews who lived in the Diaspora. It is very likely that, using the parallelism of ancient Hebrew poetry, he added this petition in order to achieve the holy number seven. This spoke very strongly to his readers, assuring them of God's power over all evil. And by adding this petition, Matthew also gave this prayer the liturgical form that a host of other Jewish prayers followed.

What did Jesus mean by *evil*? At the time He taught the disciples this prayer, the notions of *evil* and *the evil one* were often used interchangeably. People thought of the latter as being the cause of the former. But we no longer regard them as practically interchangeable. The development of science and technology has created a whole new paradigm for the interpretation of events that in the past were considered either miracles of God or the work of demons. For example, we now explain in biological and physical terms many diseases that in former times were considered the work of the forces of evil. The same applies to wars, famines, floods, and other catastrophes. Therefore, it seems worthwhile to distinguish between evil and the evil one, between something that we experience in us and around us and those "principalities and powers in the heavenly places" (Ephesians 3:10). Today, we see evil not only in the personalities behind the terms *devil, Satan, Beelzebul, demon,* and *legion,* but also in the things represented by terms such as *greed, thirst for power,*

*blind ambition, corruption, prejudice, bias, egotism, chauvinism, national-
ism, racism, more profit,* and *selfishness.*

One way of stating it is that evil is simply the absence of good, as
darkness is the absence of light and sin is the absence of love. If we love
God, we keep His commandments (John 14:15). If we love the light and
walk in it, darkness is not in us (1 John 1:5–7). And if we love the good
and do it, God abides in us and love is perfected in us (1 John 3:16–18;
4:8–21), then there's no room for evil.

In other words, evil isn't something that exists in and by itself. It certainly isn't a power of equal standing and strength with God, as portrayed in dualistic forms of religion, such as that of the ancient Persians.
Evil is nothing! It appears only in the form of the absence of good. So
when we pray for God to save us from evil, our prayer means, "Hallowed
be Thy name; Thy kingdom come, Thy will be done." Wherever God's
name is sanctified, wherever His will is done, and wherever His kingdom
is realized, evil disappears. And conversely, it is precisely in the absence
of these realizations of God's kingdom and the accomplishment of His
will that evil exists. So evil is the result not only of human or demonic
actions but also of human *inaction*—of negligence on our part to do
good, to love our neighbor, and to strive toward the realization of the
kingdom of God in our lives. When we pray the Lord's Prayer, we're
crying to God, our heavenly Father, to bring about the realization of His
kingdom and thereby deliver us from evil.

"Lead us not into a foreign village"

Some words are more difficult to translate than others. The concept of
temptation was one of those very difficult terms for which there was no
functional equivalent in the language of the people of the Tor. They were
acquainted with notions of trying, proving, or testing, but not the notion
of "inciting to evil" in a moral sense. So for a number of years, they
prayed for deliverance from evil forces, such as famine, floods, earthquakes, and diseases. Later, they also began to petition for protection

from war, greed, jealousy, selfishness, lust for power, curses and evil spells, revenge, and the destruction exercised by their gods.

Then one day, Kaway, a man of few words but remarkable insight both linguistically and otherwise, came up with the idea they should pray, "Lead us not into a foreign village." At first, I didn't quite understand his reasoning, but then it clicked.

The people of the Tor lived in small and very isolated villages. Each village constituted a world of its own, with its own social organization, culture, religion, and even language. Often the population of a village constituted also a whole tribe, though it might consist of only some one hundred and fifty people. Contacts between these village tribes consisted of *silent trade*—a form of commerce, hostile incursions into each others' territories to hunt or fish or to abduct women and girls, and wars that were the result of these incursions. Even the silent trade was dangerous. At any time, someone could become angry and shoot an arrow into the other traders' camp.

Sometimes, however, men from differing tribes happened to meet under none of these circumstances. The first thing they must do when that happened was to take a betel nut from the small net that they wore around their neck and exchange it for one from the other person. Then they would share with each other the lime they carried in their cylindrical earlobe containers and say, *"Nogookwabaay."* ("Now we can talk with each other.") No conversation—let alone relationship—could develop without the sharing of betel nuts, lime, and sirih leaves.

The use of betel nut all over New Guinea, Melanesia, Polynesia, and Micronesia is rooted in symbolism. The sacred stories of the people of these regions spell out how the betel nut came to them and how and when it should be used. The sharing of betel nut facilitated communication, trust, peace negotiations, sexual relations, and communication with the gods and with the dead. It was rooted in the whole social and religious life of those people.

However, betel nut has a mild sedative effect on people, leads to infections in the hollow of the mouth, and may become addictive. Consequently, many mission organizations have forbidden their members to use betel nuts in the same way that they forbid the use of alcohol, drugs, and tobacco. But because of how deeply the use of betel nut has permeated the culture, one can imagine how difficult it was for these people to give it up.

When the Bora-Bora accepted the good news of the gospel and decided to destroy their sacred house with its sacred flutes and other symbols, they felt compelled to share the new joy and certainties they had found with all the other tribes in the area. It was this mission that brought them the new understanding of temptation. They had all agreed not to use betel nuts any longer. That was quite a sacrifice on their part, and it led to a number of unexpected changes in their social life. It posed an additional problem when they went to the other villages on their mission. There would be no talking, no communication, no building of a relationship of trust, no sharing of the good news without first sharing betel nuts together—something they had decided not to do. The temptation to fall back into using betel nut was heightened by the good purpose that would be served if they did so.

So, for them, *temptation* meant being put, or putting themselves, in a position where they couldn't refuse to participate in something that they knew was wrong. What a powerful insight! Their prayer, then, was for God to help them find a way out of this situation so they wouldn't succumb to the power of culture and traditions. *"Taminakabka abasa aaftifahreean narem yamina wayakena amestenooni."* ("Lead us in such a way that we don't have to do what we aren't supposed to do.")

A cry for redemption

The cry for redemption from evil is a cry that affects us all. It affects those who for one reason or another, whether or not they have chosen it, have been put in a position of immense suffering, disappointment, depression, poverty, oppression, or tyranny. We are powerless against the circumstances that shape our lives so negatively. We may blame genetic disorders or family conditions, economic forces or power structures, but there's little or nothing we can do about them.

We face two temptations here. On the one hand, we can choose to fight with all our might against the bad conditions and evil structures. People everywhere make that choice, and understandably so. But that choice leads only to failure and frustration.

On the other hand, we may give up—simply resign ourselves to the inevitable. To both groups of people the Lord's Prayer offers another way, a better way. God is aware of our sufferings. He hears our cries, and He cares about us. He is our Father, and He wants only the best for us; He wants us to be well.

No, He doesn't do away with all suffering and pain—not immediately at least. But we can pray that His will be accomplished and His kingdom be realized in our lives and in our time. The cry for redemption then becomes a cry for the restoration of God's kingdom. In fact, only those who have suffered evil can cry out from experience and with conviction for the restoration of God's kingdom and the doing of His will.

It is the coming of our Lord Jesus Christ that will bring about the fulfillment of these prayers. From its beginning to its end, the Lord's Prayer is a cry for our Lord to come soon to establish His reign of righteousness and love where there will be no more evil, no more pain, and even death itself will have been destroyed. Then He will create a new heaven and a new earth where the only part of the Lord's Prayer we will pray will be "Abba, Father, hallowed be Thy name!"

Yes, come, Lord Jesus.

For Further Reflection

1. When Jesus taught His disciples to pray, " 'Lead us not into temptation,' " He Himself had endured many serious temptations, and "because he himself has suffered and been tempted, he is able to help those who are tempted" (Hebrews 2:18). How do the Gospels describe those temptations of Jesus? (Matthew 4:1–11; 16:22–24; 27:39–44, among other biblical passages).

2. How is evil related to the presence and work of Satan, "the evil one," the devil? Is all evil the result of Satan's instigation, or does it also exist apart from him?

3. What did Jesus mean by the words, " 'Watch and pray that you may not enter into temptation; the spirit indeed is willing, but the flesh is weak' " (Mark 14:38)? What are the main sources of the temptations believers face on their Christian pilgrimage?

4. What kind of temptations do followers of Christ often face when they are involved in Christ's work of making God's name known in all the world and are participating in His mission of making the kingdom of God a reality on earth?

5. What counsel does the Bible offer us regarding the fight to overcome evil? What special means and instruments has God made available to us?

FOR THINE IS THE KINGDOM . . .

The early Christian church absorbed the Lord's Prayer and responded to it with a statement of thanksgiving and praise—the doxology "for Thine is the kingdom, and the power, and the glory. Amen." Christ may not have spoken these words—the oldest and most reliable manuscripts of the New Testament don't include them. But this doxology does represent an authentic response of the early church to Jesus' prayer, and, as such, it functions as a model for our own response.

Our response centers in the belief that through Christ our Lord, we have received the redemption of our sins, a whole new relationship with God (whom we may address as "Daddy"), and the assurance that His reign will soon be an accomplished fact in all the world. Only a little while longer and all of God's creatures—on earth as well as in the heavens—will live by the principles that represent God's design for the world. The whole of God's creation—even the animals—will share in this glorious change.

Besides a response of praise, the doxology is also a response of commitment on the part of those who pray it, whether in concert with other believers or alone. In praying this prayer, people are committing themselves to help bring about the realization of the kingdom of God and the fulfillment of His will. No one can honestly and with conviction pray

"Thy will be done" without committing themselves to the salvation of people who have never heard the gospel. And no one can conscientiously pray for the restoration of God's kingdom and for delivery from evil without participating in word and deed in their realization in all the world.

So the Lord's Prayer—and this may be said of all prayers—demands both *praise* and *participation*. Prayers that don't include praise of God tend to become self-absorbed and to focus on our own needs and wants. When we don't praise God for His goodness and love, power and glory, we more easily become disappointed when some of our requests seem to go unanswered. Praising God assures us that He will, indeed, give us anything we ask for in His name.

Participation in what we pray shows that we are authentic in our praying. We know that we can't contribute anything to our own salvation or that of others; all is by God's grace. Yet when we praise God for the great sacrifice He made at the Cross, we thereby "no longer live for [ourselves] but for him who . . . died and was raised" (2 Corinthians 5:15). Praying with Christ "Thy kingdom come" makes us all both citizens and ambassadors for Christ, who has given us the ministry of reconciliation (2 Corinthians 5:18–20). Praising God for His power means that we recognize that we ourselves are empowered thereby and thus are committed to " 'go . . . and make disciples of all nations, baptizing them in the name of the Father and of the Son and of the Holy Spirit, teaching them to observe all that I have commanded you' " (Matthew 28:18–20).

Prayer that doesn't include praise to God and participation in His mission of reconciliation is like faith without works: it is dead. It remains ineffective and superficial, empty and without reward. The Lord's Prayer, therefore, includes praise of God for His goodness and mercy, His care and Fatherly love. It is this love, in turn, that compels us—that leaves us no other choice but to participate in Christ's work of establishing His kingdom in all the world. And we do so with *perseverance* (1 Thessalonians 5:17).

Praise, participation, and perseverance: these constitute the means through which we accomplish the mission the Lord's Prayer has given us.

Forever

It is difficult to imagine what *forever* means. We are constantly caught up in cascades of changes. Everything in us and around us is in a constant flux of growth and development, decline, decay, and disappearance. As the saying goes, "The only thing that doesn't change is change itself." Empires have come and gone. Kingdoms have blossomed and then disappeared. Cultures have developed and then declined. Nothing seems permanent. Everything is constantly in transition. Even we human beings are like the grass in the field.

Over and against this impermanence of our earthly existence stands the kingdom of God. It will last forever. So will God's honor and glory, His covenant and His law, His justice and redemption, His power and His love. And in His kingdom, life itself will last forever. Death will be no more, and the redeemed will reign as kings in all eternity (Revelation 22:5).

To the people of the Tor, the notion of eternity was so new that the only way they could express it in their language was by taking a deep breath, holding it, and then slowly releasing it while saying *"Gooynemera-a-a-a-a-a-a-a."* The longer one could hold one's breath, the longer the word would become—and the deeper their expression of eternity. So simple. And yet so profound. We ourselves cannot fathom it, and we gasp for air when we think of a reign and a love that will last forever.

Amen

The word *amen* has a long history. It was used in ancient times to affirm an important decree or proclamation. It meant something such as "this we truly believe," "this is indeed how it is," "so be it in truth." In Israel, it also was used as a personal affirmation, a statement of consent, a promise to abide by what was being proclaimed; so it also meant "it shall truly be accomplished," "we promise that we shall do it," "we shall abide by it." (There's that commitment aspect again!) Putting it all together then, *amen* means "we accept the premises of this statement [blessing or prayer] and shall act accordingly. You can rely on that!"

Jesus Himself often began His teaching with the words *amen, amen,* which are translated in our Bibles as "truly" or "verily" (see, for example, Mark 3:28; Luke 12: 44; 21:3). In doing so, He was both testifying to the veracity of what He was teaching and also urging His audiences to make this teaching their own. He wanted them to accept it as the truth but also to live by it—to make it their own statement of faith and principle. So, placing this term at the end of the Lord's Prayer is fully in harmony with both Jewish prayer practices at the time of Jesus and with Jesus' intention that we make this prayer our very own and practice it.

Pray without ceasing

It is true that praying the Lord's Prayer demands that we understand what Jesus meant when He taught us this prayer. Without that understanding, our recitation of the prayer tends to become formulaic. It leads to superficiality—a vain repetition of words that doesn't inspire anyone to commitment. So understanding the Lord's Prayer requires a study of God's Word in the setting in which this prayer has come to us. Such a study is all the more necessary as it is these Scriptures that testify of Jesus and of His message (John 5:39).

It is also true that merely knowing the words that comprise the Lord's Prayer and their meaning and background won't enable us to fully understand the meaning of this prayer. We must meditate upon those words and experience them in the setting of our own lives and the places where God has put us. Then the words Jesus taught us will become *our* words; His thoughts, *our* thoughts, and His mind, *our* mind!

To arrive at a deep understanding of the Lord's Prayer, we must also open our minds and hearts to the workings of the Holy Spirit. As Jesus has told us, " 'These things I have spoken to you, while I am still with you. But the Counselor, the Holy Spirit, whom the Father will send in my name, he will teach you all things, and bring to your remembrance all that I have said to you' " (John 14:25, 26; see also 16:7–15).

Finally, understanding the Lord's Prayer requires that we pray it without ceasing, in season and out of season (cf. 1 Thessalonians 5:17). Learning how to pray is like learning how to swim. One can study all the body movements in great detail. One can even practice them on the beach. But it isn't until one hits the water that one can learn how to swim. To understand the Lord's Prayer, we must take the plunge and practice praying it in the understanding we have gained through Bible study, meditation, and the influence of the Holy Spirit. That kind of praying will effectively bring about what we ask God for. Jesus promised, " 'Truly, truly, I say to you, he who believes in me will also do the works that I do; and greater works than these will he do, because I go to the Father. Whatever you ask in my name, I will do it, that the Father may be glorified in the Son; if you ask anything in my name, I will do it' " (John 14:12–14).

Praying the Lord's Prayer in all the depth of its meaning and with the commitment it calls for will bring about the realization of the kingdom of God, the accomplishment of God's will, the defeat of the last vestiges of all evil, the end of all sickness and death, hunger and disease, and the full revelation of the sons and daughters of God. However, though clearly a mark of identity and a confession of faith, a mandate and road map for mission, a source of power and a unifying force amidst the diversity of believers, the Lord's Prayer is first and foremost a prayer. Therein lies its power to sustain and comfort believers, to help them on their life's journey, to keep them in the faith, and to empower them participate with Christ in bringing about the kingdom of God in our time.

Nobody who receives this prayer in the meaning in which it was given and conscientiously prays it in the mind of Christ will fail to experience its powerful effects in his or her life. Whole churches, too, may be rejuvenated by a renewed understanding of this prayer. Let us therefore pray it individually and communally "without ceasing."

For Further Reflection

1. How do the message and mission given us in the Lord's Prayer relate to the everlasting gospel and to the three angels' messages of Revelation 14:6–12?

2. According to the Lord's Prayer, what is the objective of all mission? What is the message to be communicated? What is the best method of reaching the objective? Who are the missionaries? And what is the source of the power necessary to accomplish the mission?

3. Why and to whom did Jesus give the Lord's Prayer? Did He give it only to the twelve disciples and the crowd who heard His sermon on the mount, or did He give it to all believers who would receive the word through the disciples, including us?

4. Did Jesus give the Lord's Prayer primarily to serve as a sacred formula and standard prayer valid for all times and cultures and occasions, or did He intend it as a model given in outline form and therefore open to adaptation as human culture and conditions change?

5. Did Jesus give the Lord's Prayer for use by individuals or use by whole congregations or both? What biblical evidence is there for your answer?

BIBLIOGRAPHY

Barth, Karl. *Prayer According to the Catechisms of the Reformation.* Philadelphia: Westminster, 1952.

Bonhoeffer, Dietrich. *The Cost of Discipleship.* New York: Macmillan, 1963.

_____. *Letters and Papers From Prison.* Enlarged ed. New York: Macmillan, 1972.

Copeland, J. Mark. *After This Manner Pray: Understanding the Power of the Lord's Prayer.* South Plainfield, N.J.: Bridge Publishing, Inc., 1992.

Davis, Thomas A. *Island of Forgotten Men.* Washington, D.C.: Review and Herald® Publishing Association, 1967.

Ebeling, Gerhard. *On Prayer: The Lord's Prayer in Today's World.* Philadelphia: Fortress, 1978.

Jeremias, Joachim. *The Prayers of Jesus: Studies in Biblical Theology.* Naperville, Ill.: Allenson, 1967.

Koerner, Reinhard. *Das Vater Unser: Spiritualitaet aus dem Gebet Jesu.* Leipzig: St. Benno, 2002.

Lochman, Jan Milic. *The Lord's Prayer.* Grand Rapids, Mich.: Eerdmans, 1990.

Lohmeyer, Ernst. *"Our Father": An Introduction to the Lord's Prayer.* New York: Harper and Row, 1965.

Keller, W. Philip. *A Layman Looks at the Lord's Prayer.* Minneapolis: World Wide Publications, 1976.

Miller, Patricia D. *They Cried to the Lord: The Form and Theology of Biblical Prayer.* Minneapolis: Fortress, 1994.

Oosterwal, Gottfried. *People of the Tor: A Cultural-Anthropological Study of the Tribes of the Tor Territory.* Assen, Netherlands: Royal Van Gorcum, 1961.

_____. *Die Papua: Von der Kultur eines Naturvolkes.* Munich: Urban, 1963.

_____. *Mission: Possible.* Nashville: Southern Publishing Association, 1972.

Schnackenburg, Rudolf. *Alles Kann Wer Glaubt.* Freiburg: Herder, 1984.

Schuermann, Heinz. *Das Gebet des Herrn als Schluessel zum Verstehen Jesu.* Leipzig: St. Benno, 1990.

Stevenson, Kenneth W. *The Lord's Prayer: A Text in Tradition.* Minneapolis: Fortress, 2004.

Thielicke, Helmut. *Das Gebet das die Welt umspannt.* Stuttgart: Quell, 1953.

White, Ellen G. *The Desire of Ages.* Mountain View, Calif.: Pacific Press® Publishing Association, 1927.

_____. *The Greatest Sermon Ever Preached.* Mountain View, Calif.: Pacific Press® Publishing Association, 1955.

Willimon, William, and Stanley Hauerwas. *Lord, Teach Us: The Lord's Prayer and the Christian Life.* Nashville: Abingdon Press, 1996.

Wills, Garry. *What Jesus Meant.* New York: Penguin Books, 2006.

Work, Telford. *Ain't Too Proud to Beg: Living Through the Lord's Prayer.* Grand Rapids, Mich.: William B. Eerdmans, 2007.